A
Short History

of the

Church of Jesus Christ of Latter-day Saints

Published by
THE CHURCH OF JESUS CHRIST
OF LATTER-DAY SAINTS

The Prophet Joseph Smith

PREFACE

●

This Short History is published to provide a brief narrative of the founding and development of the Church of Jesus Christ of Latter-day Saints. In a work so limited only items of general interest and importance have been presented. For those who seek a wider knowledge of the subject there are available a number of reliable histories and commentaries.

The manuscript was prepared for the Committee chiefly by John Henry Evans to whom appreciation is due. Acknowledgment is also made to Gordon B. Hinckley for contributions to and editing of the manuscript.

That this small volume may prove an interesting story as well as a convenient reference work is the sincere desire of those responsible for it.

CHURCH RADIO, PUBLICITY AND
MISSION LITERATURE COMMITTEE

CONTENTS

●

CONTENTS

•

ILLUSTRATIONS

●

Chapter I

THE FIRST RELIGIOUS EXPERIENCE OF JOSEPH SMITH

There lived in the township of Manchester, New York, in the year 1820, a family by the name of Smith. Manchester is in the western part of the state, about twenty miles from the city of Rochester.

At this time the family comprised the father, the mother, and eight children. The father's name was Joseph; the mother's, Lucy; and the children's, in the order of their birth, Alvin, Hyrum, Sophronia, Joseph, Samuel H., William, Catherine and Don Carlos. Alvin was twenty-two years old and Don Carlos, six. Two other children were born to this couple—Ephraim in 1810, who lived but eleven days, and Lucy in 1821.

The Smiths, however, had not always lived in this part of the country. With seven children the parents had come to New York State in the year 1815 from the border line of Vermont and New Hampshire.

When the elder Joseph Smith's first American ancestor, Robert Smith, came to America in 1638 from near London, England, he settled in Massachusetts. Lucy Smith's first American forebear, John Mack, came from Inverness, Scotland, arriving in Boston in 1680. Later, with his wife, he settled in Connecticut. In time, however, the Smiths found their way to Vermont, and the Macks to New Hampshire. Joseph and Lucy met while the young woman was on a visit to her brother, who lived in the same town as the Smiths.

In the main the progenitors of both the Smiths and the Macks were farm folk, although among the former there was a member of Congress and among

the latter a clergyman. In the main, too, the members
of both families were orthodox Christians. However,
they were not, generally speaking, unthinking believers,
and some of them were outspoken in their opposition
to some practices of the church. But, one and all,
they believed in God and in the immortality of the
soul.

On the marriage of Joseph Smith and Lucy Mack
in January, 1796, Lucy's brother and his business
partner gave her a thousand dollars as a wedding
present. The couple lived on their own farm
in the township of Tunbridge, Vermont, and kept a
small store. But reverses came, first in business
and then in farming; a drouth visited the region for
three years in succession. The result was that they
moved to the western part of New York State, then
much advertised as a new and promising part of the
United States. There they were compelled to make
a fresh start under somewhat adverse conditions.

Their first home was in Palmyra. Here they
remained for four years. All the members of the
family who were able to do so, worked to support
themselves and to lay by something with which to
buy a farm on the outskirts of the town. At the end
of the four years they moved upon some land which
they had purchased in the neighboring township of
Manchester. From this they cleared the timber and
underbrush, planted crops, and built a two story log
house.

* * * * *

Joseph Smith, Jun., was born on the twenty-
third of December, 1805, while the family lived in
Sharon, Vermont. In the year 1820, he was therefore in his fifteenth year.

In person he was an attractive boy. He was
large for his age, with light hair and light eyebrows

and eyelashes. His nose was large, and his eyes, hazel in color, were rather deep set. In later years men spoke of his eyes as being penetrating.

Even in his youth he was of a meditative disposition. So his mother says. He liked to think things out for himself. He was never a great reader, although very early he learned to read, to write, and to figure. He had gone to school perhaps as much as the average boy of his time. There are still extant three books which he used in the school at Palmyra.

In personality he was attractive. His disposition was cheery and jovial. He liked people and people liked him.

These traits, physicial and mental, characterized him all his life.

His home was a religious home. Its atmosphere was Christian, although in 1820 none of the family belonged to any church. In this home the Bible was read with interest as the Word of God; there was frequent, if not daily, prayer; and a blessing was asked on the meal before it was partaken of. Besides, the members of the family tried to do what they thought was right by one another and by their neighbors. They were industrious, thrifty, and passionately fond of one another.

* * * * *

"Some time in the second year after our removal to Manchester," says the Prophet in his *Autobiography*, "there was in the place where we lived an unusual excitement on the subject of religion. It commenced with the Methodists, but soon became general among all the sects in that region. Indeed, the whole district seemed affected by it, and great multitudes united themselves to the different religious parties. This created no small stir and divisions among the people, sqme crying, 'Lo here!' and others, 'Lo, there!' Some were contending for the Methodist faith, some for the Presbyterian, and some for the Baptist.

"For notwithstanding the great love which the converts to these different faiths expressed at the time of their conversion and the great zeal manifested by the respective clergy, yet when the converts began to file off, some to one party and some to another, it was seen that the seemingly good feelings of both the priests and the converts were more pretended than real. A scene of the greatest confusion and bad feeling ensued; priest contending against priest and convert against convert; so that all their good feelings for one another were entirely lost in a strife of words and a contest about opinions.

"During this time of great excitement my mind was called up to serious reflection and great uneasiness; but though my feelings were deep and often poignant, still I kept myself aloof from all these parties, though I attended their several meetings as often as occasion would permit. In process of time my mind became somewhat partial to the Methodist sect, and I felt a desire to be united with them. But so great were the confusion and strife among the different denominations, that it was impossible for a person young as I was and so unacquainted with men and things, to come to any certain conclusion who was right and who was wrong.

"In the midst of this war of words and tumult of opinions, I often said to myself, What is to be done? Who of all these parties are right? Or are they all wrong together? If any one of them be right, which is it and how shall I know it? While I was laboring under the extreme difficulties caused by the contests of these parties of religionists, I was one day reading the epistle of James (1-5,) which reads: 'If any of you lack wisdom, let him ask of God, that giveth to all men liberally, and upbraideth not; and it shall be given him.'

"Never did any passage of scripture come with more power to the heart of man than this did at this time to mine. It seemed to enter with great force into every feeling of my heart. I reflected on it again and again, knowing that if any person needed wisdom from God, I did; for how to act I did not know, and unless I could get more wisdom than I then had, I would never know. For the teachers of religion understood the same passage of scripture so differently as to destroy all confidence in settling the question by an appeal to the Bible.

"At length I came to the conclusion to 'ask of God,' concluding that if he gave wisdom to them that lacked wisdom, and would give liberally and not upbraid, I might venture. So, in accordance with this, my determination, I retired to the woods to make the attempt.

"It was on the morning of a beautiful, clear day, early in the spring of 1820. It was the first time in my life that I had made such an attempt. After I had retired to the place where I had previously designed to go, having looked around me and finding myself alone, I kneeled down and began to offer up the desires of my heart to God.

"I had scarcely done so, when immediately I was seized upon by some power which entirely overcame me, and had such an astonishing influence over me as to bind my tongue so that I could not speak. Thick darkness gathered round me, and it seemed to me for a time as if I were doomed to sudden destruction. But, exerting all my powers to call upon God to deliver me from this enemy, and at the very moment when I was ready to sink into despair and abandon myself to destruction, I saw a pillar of light exactly

over my head, above the brightness of the sun, which
descended gradually until it fell upon me.

"It no sooner appeared than I found myself delivered from the enemy which had held me bound.
When the light rested upon me, I saw two personages,
whose brightness and glory defy all description, standing above me in the air. One of them spake unto
me, calling me by name, and said, pointing to the
other, 'This is my beloved Son; hear him.'

"My object in going to inquire of the Lord was to
know which of all the sects was right, that I might
know which to join. No sooner, therefore, did I get
possession of myself, so as to be able to speak, than
I asked the personages who stood above me in the
light, which of all the sects was right and which I
should join.

"I was answered that I must join none of them,
for they were all wrong; and the personage who addressed me said that all their creeds were an abom-
ination in his sight. 'They draw near to me with their
lips, but their hearts are far from me; they teach
for doctrines the commandments of men, having a
form of godliness but they deny the power thereof.'
And many other things did he say unto me, which I
cannot write at this time.

"Some few days after I had had this vision,
I happened to be in company with one of the Methodist
preachers, who was very active in the before-men-
tioned religious excitement, and conversing with him
on the subject of religion I took occasion to give him
an account of the vision which I had had. I was
greatly surprised at his behavior; he treated my communication not only lightly, but with great contempt,
saying, it was all of the devil, that there were no such
things as visions or revelations in these days; that all
such things had ceased with the apostles and that there
would never be any more of them.

"I soon found, however, that my telling the story

had excited a great deal of prejudice against me among professors of religion, and was the cause of great persecution, which continued to increase; and though I was an obscure boy, only between fourteen and fifteen years of age, and my circumstances in life such as to make a boy of no consequence in the world, yet men of high standing would take notice sufficient to excite the public mind against me, and create a bitter persecution; and this was common among all the sects —all united to persecute me.

"It caused me serious reflection then, and often has since, how very strange it was that an obscure boy should be thought a character of sufficient importance to attract the attention of the great ones of the most popular sects of the day, and in a manner to create in them a spirit of the most bitter persecution and reviling. But strange or not, so it was, and it was often the cause of great sorrow to myself.

"However, it was nevertheless a fact that I had beheld a vision. I had actually seen a light, and in the midst of that light I saw two personages, and they did in reality speak to me; and though I was hated and persecuted for saying that I had seen a vision, yet it was true; and while they were persecuting me, reviling me, and speaking all manner of evil against me falsely for so saying, I was led to say in my heart, Why persecute me for telling the truth? I have actually seen a vision, and who am I that I can withstand God, or why does the world think to make me deny what I have actually seen? For I had seen a vision; I knew it, and I knew that God knew it, and I could not deny it, neither dared I do it.

"I had now got my mind satisfied so far as the sectarian world was concerned; that it was not my duty to join with any of them, but to continue as I was until further directed. I had found the testimony of James to be true, that a man who lacked wisdom might ask of God, and obtain, and not be upbraided."

Chapter II

A SERIES OF SPIRITUAL EXPERIENCES

Beginning with September 21, 1823, Joseph Smith had a series of spiritual manifestations from heaven. This was after an interval of about three and a half years from the time of the first manifestation. As in the other case it is best to have the story of these revelations in his own language, slightly abridged. He says:

"During the space of time which intervened between the time I had the vision and the year 1823, I was left to all kinds of temptations; and, mingling with all kinds of society, I frequently fell into foolish errors, and displayed the weakness of youth and the foibles of human nature, which, I am sorry to say, led me into divers temptations, offensive in the sight of God.

"In making this confession, no one need suppose me guilty of any great or malignant sins. A disposition to commit such was never in my nature. But I was guilty of levity, and sometimes associated with jovial company, not consistent with that character which ought to be maintained by one who was called of God as I had been.

"In consequence of these things, I often felt condemned for my weakness and imperfections, when, on the evening of the above mentioned twenty-first of September, after I had retired to my bed for the night, I betook myself to prayer and supplication to Almighty God for forgiveness of all my sins and follies, and also for a manifestation to me, that I might know of my state before him. For I had confidence in obtaining a divine manifestation.

"While I was thus in the act of calling upon God, I discovered a light appearing in my room, which continued to increase until the room was lighter than at noonday, when immediately a personage appeared at my bedside, standing in the air, for his feet did not touch the floor.

"He had on a loose robe of most exquisite whiteness. It was a whiteness beyond anything earthly I had ever seen; nor do I believe that any earthly thing could be made to appear so exceedingly white and brilliant. His hands were naked, and his arms also, a little above the wrist; so, also, were his feet naked, as were his legs, a little above the ankles. His head and neck were also bare. I could discover that he had no other clothing on but this robe, as it was open, so that I could see into his bosom. Not only was his robe exceedingly white, but his whole person was glorious beyond description, and his countenance truly like lightning. The room was exceedingly light, but not so very bright as immediately around his person.

"When I first looked upon him, I was afraid; but the fear soon left me. He called me by name, and said unto me that he was a messenger sent from the presence of God, and that his name was Moroni; that God had a work for me to do; and that my name should be had for good and evil among all nations, kindreds, and tongues. He said there was a book deposited, written upon gold plates, giving an account of the former inhabitants of this (the American) continent, and the source from whence they sprang. He also said that the fulness of the Gospel was contained in it, as delivered by the Savior to the ancient inhabitants; also that there were two stones in silver bows—and these stones, fastened to a breastplate, constituted what is called the Urim and Thummim—deposited with the plates; and the possession and use of these stones were what constituted 'seers' in ancient times; and that God had prepared them for the purpose of translating the book.

"He told me, that when I got those plates, I should not show them to any person; neither the breastplate with the Urim and Thummim—only to those to whom I should be commanded to show them. If I did, I should be destroyed. While he was conversing with me about the plates, the vision was opened to my mind that I could see the place where the plates were deposited.

"After this communication I saw the light in the room begin to gather immediately around the person of him who had been speaking to me, and it continued to do so until the room was again left dark, except just around him, when instantly I saw, as it were, a conduit open right up into heaven, and he ascended until he entirely disappeared, and the room was left as it had been before this heavenly light had made its appearance.

"I lay musing on the singularity of the scene and marveling greatly at what had been told me by this extraordinary messenger, when, in the midst of my meditation, I suddenly discovered that my room was again beginning to get lighted, and in an instant, as it were, the same heavenly messenger was again by my bedside. He again related the very same things which he had done at the first visit, without the least variation. Having related these things, he again ascended as he had done before.

"By this time, so deep were the impressions made on my mind, that sleep had fled from my eyes, and I lay overwhelmed in astonishment at what I had both seen and heard. But what was my surprise when again I beheld the same messenger at my bedside, and heard him repeat over again to me the same things as before; and added a caution that Satan would try to tempt me (in consequence of the indigent circumstances of my father's family,) to get the plates for the purpose of geting rich. This he forbade me.

"After this third visit, he again ascended into heaven as before, and I was again left to ponder on the strangeness of what I had just experienced. Almost immediately after the heavenly messenger had ascended from me the third time, the cock crowed, and I found that the day was approaching; so that our interviews must have occupied the whole of that night.

* * * * *

"I shortly after arose from my bed, and, as usual, went to the necessary labors of the day; but, in attempting to work as at other times, I found my strength so exhausted as to render me entirely unable. My father, who was laboring along with me, discovered something to be wrong with me, and told me to go home. I started with the intention of going to the house; but, in attempting to cross the fence out of the field where we were, my strength entirely failed me, and I fell helpless on the ground, and for a time was quite unconscious of anything.

"The first thing that I can recollect was a voice speaking unto me, calling me by name. I looked up and beheld the same messenger standing over my head, surrounded by light as before. He then again related unto me all that he had related to me the previous night, and commanded me to go to my father and tell him of the vision and commandment which I had received. I returned to my father in the field, and rehearsed the whole matter to him. He replied to me that it was of God, and told me go and do as commanded by the messenger. I left the field and went to the place where the messenger had told me the plates were deposited; and, owing to the distinctness of the vision which I had had concerning it, I knew the place the instant that I arrived there.

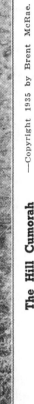

The Hill Cumorah —Copyright 1935 by Brent McRae.

"Convenient to the village of Manchester stands a hill of considerable size, and the most elevated of any in the neighborhood. On the west side of this hill, not far from the top, under a stone of considerable size, lay the plates, deposited in a stone box. This stone was thick and rounding in the middle on the upper side, and thinner towards the edges, so that the middle part of it was visible above the ground, but the edge all round was covered with earth.

"Having removed the earth, I obtained a lever, which I got fixed under the edge of the stone, and, with a little exertion, raised it up. I looked in, and there indeed did I behold the plates, the Urim and Thummim, and the breastplate, as stated by the messenger. The box in which they lay was formed by laying stones together in some kind of cement. In the bottom of the box were laid two stones crossways of the box, and on these stones lay the plates and the other things with them.

"I made an attempt to take them out, but was forbidden by the messenger, and was again informed that the time for bringing them forth had not yet arrived, neither would it, until four years from that time. But he told me that I should come to that place precisely in one year from that time, and that he would there meet with me, and that I should continue to do so until the time should come for obtaining the plates.

"Accordingly, I went at the end of each year, and at each time I found the same messenger there, and received instruction and intelligence from him at each of our interviews, respecting what the Lord was going to do, and how and in what manner his kingdom was to be conducted in the last days.

"At length the time arrived for obtaining the plates, the Urim and Thummim, and the breastplate. On the twenty-second day of September, 1827, having gone as usual at the end of another year to the place where they were deposited, the same heavenly messenger delivered them up to me, with this charge: That I should be responsible for them; that if I should let them go carelessly, or through any neglect of mine, I should be cut off; but that if I would use all my endeavors to preserve them until he, the messenger, should call for them, they should be protected.

"I soon found out the reason why I had received such strict charges to keep them safe, and why it was that the messenger had said that when I had done what was required at my hand, he would call for them. For, no sooner was it known that I had them, than the most strenuous exertions were used to get them from me. But by the wisdom of God, they remained safe in my hands until I had accomplished by them what was required. When, according to arrangements, the messenger called for them, I delivered them up to him."

Chapter III

THE GOLD PLATES AND THE BOOK
OF MORMON

The ancient record proved an interesting volume. Each plate was about seven inches in width by about eight inches in length, and about the thickness of common tin. On both sides were beautiful engravings. How many plates there were we do not know. They were bound together into a book of about six inches in thickness, by three rings running through the plates on one side of the volume. Approximately one-third of the book, however, was "sealed," so that no one might read the contents. This is the explanation of the phrase in the testimony of the Eight Witnesses: "as many of the leaves as the said Smith has translated we did handle with our hands." According to the record itself, the language was akin to Hebrew.

On receiving the plates Joseph Smith with all diligence sought to keep them from falling into the hands of those who would not regard them as sacred.

Apparently the whole countryside was aroused over what the Smiths had said about the visions by one of the family. Joseph, as we have seen, told a Methodist minister about his first religious experience. No doubt others, too, came to know about it. One gathers, particularly from the account of Mother Smith, that the neighbors, near and far, knew the story of the heavenly messenger and the gold plates. Joseph shortly found himself singled out for unfavorable attention from his fellow townsmen, young and old. The Prophet's phrase in his account is significant: "No sooner was it known that I had them (the plates) than the most strenuous exertions were used to get them from me."

For some time the Smiths were hard pressed to
find a place to hide the book. The hollow trunk of an
old birch tree in the woods, the floor of a carpenter's
shop across the road from the home, the hearth under
a stone taken out for the purpose, and later a keg of
beans—these, in turn, became the hiding place of the
golden volume. Every once in a while groups of
neighbors, sometimes led by a diviner, made raids on
the Smith premises, to try to locate it.

*   *   *   *   *

The constant annoyance to which the young prophet was subjected in his home town prompted him
to look about for a more peaceful place in which to
translate. In January of this year (1827) he had
married Emma Hale, the attractive daughter of Isaac
Hale, of Harmony (now Oakland), Pennsylvania. The
occasion of his going to Harmony in the first place
was as a laborer for Josiah Stoal, a good friend of
the Smith family. Stoal owned an old Spanish mine
in the neighborhood of the Hale residence. It was
to Harmony, therefore, that he went, in December
of this year. Martin Harris, a well-to-do farmer near
Manchester, who had become greatly interested in
Joseph's religious work, gave him fifty dollars for the
journey. Emma's brother came from Pennsylvania to
Manchester and took the couple to Harmony. For
the next year and a half Harmony was the Prophet's
home. He bought some land from his father-in-law,
which he tilled himself, and a yoke of oxen from
Josiah Stoal.

Arrived at Harmony, Joseph "commenced copy-
ing the characters off the plates, and, by means of
the Urim and Thummim, translated some of them."
This he did between the time of his coming to the home
of his father-in-law, in December of this year, and the
following February.

The man who acted as scribe for the Prophet

during the translation of the *Book of Mormon* as we
have it now, was Oliver Cowdery.   Cowdery was a
school teacher.   He had taught in Manchester during
the winter of 1828-29.   He was ten months the junior
of the Prophet.   A highly intelligent young man,
Oliver had had considerable schooling for those times.
As was the custom then, he had boarded among the

Oliver Cowdery

families that had
children i n h i s
school.   It w a s
while he boarded
with   the   Smiths
that he learned of
Joseph's   visions.
He became greatly
interested.   After
talking   with   his
friend David Whit-
mer   about   these
visions, Oliver de-
cided to pay a visit
to the Prophet, in
Harmony, and, if
he found the facts
to be as he had
been led to believe,
he would remain to
write for him. One
thing   that   prob-
ably helped him to
make up his mind
that Joseph was
really a seer, is recorded in a revelation to the Prophet,
in which Cowdery was told something that only he
could have known.   At any rate, Oliver wrote to his
friend David that he "had revealed knowledge concerning the truth of" the gold plates.   So he stayed

to write for the Prophet. This was the first time the two had met.

On the seventh of April, 1829, the translation of the ancient record was again taken up. And it progressed now without interruption, till the task was finished some time in June—a period of about three months. Thus the principal obstacle to the literary labor of the Prophet was removed. Removed also was the financial obstacle. For Joseph's former employer, Joseph Knight, a well-to-do farmer and grist mill owner at Colesville, New York, brought supplies of provisions to the two workers—a distance of more than a hundred miles.

The work, however, was not completed in Harmony, but in Fayette, New York. Toward the end of the task, some opposition arose in Harmony. At first Isaac Hale, Joseph's father-in-law, took sides with the translators, but later grew tired of defending them. So the Prophet deemed it advisable to accept an invitation extended by the Whitmers, in Fayette, to live with them till the translation was finished. David Whitmer went for Joseph, Oliver and Emma. This was some time in June, 1829.

After the change of residence, the work progressed very rapidly. The Prophet kept at the laborious task almost continuously, while his regular scribe was relieved by Emma and various members of the Whitmer family.

A question is often asked as to the manner of translation. There are many points which we cannot now answer, but the following description may be depended upon: First, a curtain separated the Prophet from his scribe. This prevented the latter from seeing the plates and the Urim and Thummim. Second, the translation of the ancient language was made by means of the Urim and Thummim, or interpreters. We learn this from both Oliver Cowdery and Joseph

Smith, the only persons in a position to know. Third, it required a mental effort to translate. This is evident from a revelation (section 9 of the *Doctrine and Covenants*) in which Oliver is informed that his failure to do some translating was due to his not having taken into account that he "must study it out in his mind." Fourth, the translation required spiritual and emotional purity, otherwise the translator could do nothing, all being "dark."

The translation completed, the next consideration was to find a publisher.

For obvious reasons the Prophet wished to employ a printer at some other town than Palmyra. So he went to Rochester, New York. But the man approached there would not undertake to put out the work. Joseph, therefore was forced to apply to the printer in Palmyra,—E. B. Grandin. A contract was entered into between Grandin and the Prophet to print five thousand copies for three thousand dollars. Since Joseph Smith had no money to pay for the printing, Martin Harris, through a mortgage on his farm raised the necessary funds.

Meantime, a copyright was secured in the name of Joseph Smith, Jun., as "author and proprietor." These words had to be used because the copyright law had then no provision for the translation of a literary work.

The book came out in March, 1830, under the title *The Book of Mormon*. The explanation of this name is simple. The plates which the Prophet translated were, for the most part, an abridgment by one named Mormon, an ancient prophet, the father of Moroni, who had lived on the American continent. Till enough copies of the book were sold to repay Martin Harris, the whole edition remained in his possession. The price per copy was two dollars and fifty cents.

Chapter IV

WITNESSES

Few literary works in any age have made such a stir in the world as the *Book of Mormon*. This is mostly due to the manner in which the book has reached us. As a religious product it is unique. Besides, so much depends on an answer to the question, Is the story of its origin true or not? For, on the one hand, if it is not true, then the entire structure of Mormonism is built on a false foundation; and, on the other hand, if it is true, it becomes the strongest physical evidence for the authenticity of Joseph Smith's story and teachings.

This is why some people spend so much of their time trying to prove that the story related by Joseph Smith as to the origin of the book is not true, and this is why, too, believers in the divine origin of the volume take such pains to show that the story is true. Involved in this controversy are essentially all the problems of the existence of spirits and angels, and also the question as to whether God is interested enough in man to reveal himself and his purposes.

It is necessary, therefore, in this chapter to go over the story of that remarkable book, the conditions under which it came forth so far as the human elements are concerned, and the evidence we have that the story of the Prophet as to its origin is true.

*   *   *   *   *

The story of the *Book of Mormon* should, alone, attract no little attention, since it is unusual in itself.

About six hundred years before Christ there lived in the city of Jerusalem a family whose father and husband, Lehi, was one of the minor prophets there, although his name does not appear in the Bible. This man, with his family and the family of another whose name was Ishmael, left the Holy City and, under divine direction, arrived in what is now known as America. The colony numbered perhaps twenty in all. With them they took some writings on brass plates—essentially the Hebrew scriptures down to the time of Jeremiah, a contemporary of Lehi.

On reaching the "Promised Land" a division occurred. Part of the colony followed Nephi, the fourth son of Lehi and a prophet; the rest adhered to Lehi's eldest son Laman, who was always a rebel at heart. For a thousand years, with intervals, these two peoples, the Nephites and the Lamanites, each occupying a separate part of the country, fought each other, the Lamanites being nearly always the aggressors.

In consequence of the possession of the scriptures and of divine guidance through prophets, the Nephites were a civilized people, and, as a result of the absence of these two things, the Lamanites were a barbarous nation. The former cultivated the art of reading and writing, and had a system of popular education. They built wooden and cement houses. They coined silver and gold into money, which they used in their commercial transactions. They had a political government, a rule of the people through judges. They erected temples and houses of worship, and had an organized church.

The Lamanites, on the other hand, had no records, for they were unable to read or write, and they had no literature generally. They built no houses, cultivated no fields or gardens, practiced the most superstitious rites in the place of revealed religion, usually ate raw meat, the fruit of the chase, painted their naked bodies, and were in general a roaming people. From the time of the arrival of the Lehites in the Promised Land to about the fourth century of the Christian Era, these two nations lived thus apart.

Some time after his resurrection Jesus Christ visited his "other sheep" mentioned in the Bible in what is now the New World. He taught them the same things, essentially, that he had taught the Jews in Palestine. Only, here he found a more acceptable frame of mind, one more receptive to the truth. Here the Church was organizd, with apostles and prophets, spiritual gifts and graces, as in the Church in Palestine. This period was the high-water mark in Lehite history. For two hundred years the two nations were one, and, like the disciples of Christ in Palestine, they "had all things common."

Meantime the Nephites, or the white people of this period in ancient America, had kept a history of their doings—as well as of the doings of their neighbors. This record was set down on plates of gold, so as to preserve the history to future generations. When the time approached for the final breakup of the united nation, one of the Nephite prophets, Mormon by name, made an abridgment of this history. This he gave to his son Moroni, to make such additions as he might see fit, then to hide it away in the earth. It was this abridgment that Moroni revealed to Joseph Smith in 1823, and finally delivered to him in 1827.

Among the things which Moroni added to the golden book intrusted to him by his father was an abridgment of what is called the book of Ether. Here is the story of Ether:

More than a thousand years before the arrival of the Lehites on the shores of what we know as America, there had come from the region of the Tower of Babel a small colony called Jaredites, named for one of their leaders, Jared. These people, also under divine direction, reached the American continent. Here they became civilized; they knew how to read and write, how to cultivate the land, to smelt ore, and to build with lumber and cement. They had a church, and through prophets and seers were blessed

with revelations of divine will. One of their prophets, the first and greatest, was the brother of Jared,
whose name was Moriancumer. In a series of revo-
lutions the Jaredites destroyed each other, till only
one man was left to tell the tale.

Interspersed with these two narratives are ex-
positions of doctrine. Practically all the main ideas
which we find in the Bible are to be found in the
Book of Mormon; only, in simpler and clearer form.
The spirit of the book is equally intense, fervent,
and spiritual as that of the Hebrew scriptures. And
it is highly moral in tone.

*   *   *   *   *

It is interesting to inquire into the purposes of
the *Book of Mormon* as given in the record itself
and in revelations to Joseph Smith.

First: On the flyleaf of the book it is stated
that the record is brought forth "to show unto the
remnant of the House of Israel what great things
the Lord hath done for their fathers; and that they
may know the covenants of the Lord, that they are
not cast off forever—and also to the convincing of
the Jew and Gentile that Jesus is the Christ, the
eternal God, manifesting himself unto all nations."
This statement, the Prophet tells us, was written
by Moroni.

Second: In section three of the *Doctrine and
Covenants,* beginning with verse 16, are these words
on the same general subject: "For inasmuch as the
knowledge of a Savior has come into the world
through the testimony of the Jews, even so shall
the knowledge of a Savior come unto my people,
and to the Nephites, and the Jacobites, and the Joseph-
ites, and the Zoramites, through the testimony of
their fathers—and this testimony shall come to the
knowledge of the Lamanites, and the Lemuelites,
and the Ishmaelites, who dwindled in unbelief because of the iniquity of their fathers, whom the Lord
has suffered to destroy their brethren the Nephites,

because of their iniquities and their abominations."

Third: In another section of the same book *(Doctrine and Covenants,* 10:62, 63) still another purpose is revealed. These verses read: "I will also bring to light my gospel which was ministered unto them [the ancient Americans], and, behold, they shall not deny that which you [Joseph Smith] have received, but they shall build it up, and *shall bring to light the true points of my doctrine,* yea the only doctrine which is in me. And this I do that I may establish my gospel, that there may not be so much contention; yea, Satan doth stir up the hearts of the people to contention concerning the points of my doctrine; and in those things they do err, for they do wrest the scriptures and do not understand them."

There was served yet another purpose. A very definite and obvious effect of the revelation of the gold plates to Joseph Smith at this particular time and the translation of them by him, was that he became familiar with the foundational truths of re-vealed religion through his literary efforts in connection with the *Book of Mormon.*

Joseph Smith at this time was not trained in theology and religion. He had read the Bible, it is true, but he was probably no better acquainted with its doctrines than the average Christian of his time. Besides, as he was to learn from the Record itself, "after the Book [the Hebrew scriptures] hath gone forth . . . many plain and precious things were taken from the book." But in the *Book of Mormon,* which was translated by direct inspiration, the doctrines of the Church of Christ were simply and clearly set forth, and in such plainness that they cannot be easily "wrested." And so, when the youthful prophet, day after day and month after month, pored over the ideas on the gold plates, he learned more thoroughly about theological and religious matters than he probably could have done in any other way.

* * * * *

There are two groups of witnesses to the Book of Mormon. One group of eight testifies to the existence of the plates from which the *Book of Mormon* was translated. This was a matter-of-fact showing of the plates by Joseph Smith to eight of his friends. Nine men met in a grove, one of them showed the golden book to the others, and these others handled this book as they would have done any other curious object, turning over the leaves and examining the characters on them. Here is their testimony:

> Be it known unto all nations, kindreds, tongues, and people, unto whom this work shall come: That Joseph Smith, Jun., the translator of this work, has shown unto us the plates of which hath been spoken, which have the appearance of gold; and as many of the leaves as the said Smith has translated we did handle with our hands; and we also saw the engravings thereon, all of which has the appearance of ancient work, and of curious workmanship.
>
> And this we bear record with words of soberness, that the said Smith has shown unto us, for we have seen and hefted, and know of a surety that the said Smith has got the plates of which we have spoken. And we give our names unto the world, to witness unto the world that which we have seen. And we lie not, God bearing witness of it.

This statement was signed by eight men: Christian Whitmer, Jacob Whitmer, Peter Whitmer, Jun., John Whitmer, Hiram Page, Joseph Smith, Sen., Hyrum Smith, and Samuel H. Smith.

Prior to this exhibition of the plates to these eight men three other men, with Joseph Smith, retired to the woods near Fayette, New York, to inquire of the Lord respecting the truth of the *Book of Mormon.* On this occasion they received the fulfillment of a promise in the record itself that three witnesses, besides "him to whom the book shall be delivered," should "behold it by the power of God." This phrase expresses the difference between the two sets of witnesses, so far as the manner of their receiving the testimony is concerned. Here is their testimony:

Be it known unto all nations, kindreds, tongues, and people, unto whom this work shall come: That we, through the grace of God the Father, and our Lord Jesus Christ, have seen the plates which contain this record, which is a record of the people of Nephi, and also of the Lamanites, their brethren, and also of the people of Jared, who came from the tower of which hath been spoken.

And we also know that they have been translated by the gift and power of God, for his voice hath declared it unto us; wherefore we know of a surety that the work is true. And we also testify that we have seen the engravings which are upon the plates; and they have been shown unto us by the power of God, and not of man.

And we declare with words of soberness, that an angel of God came down from heaven, and he brought and laid before our eyes, that we beheld and saw the plates, and the engravings thereon; and we know that it is by the grace of God the Father, and our Lord Jesus Christ, that we beheld and bear record that these things are true.

And it is marvelous in our eyes. Nevertheless, the voice of the Lord commanded us that we should bear record of it; wherefore, to be obedient unto the commandments of God, we bear testimony of these things. And we know that if we are faithful in Christ, we shall rid our garments of the blood of all men, and be found spotless before the judgment-seat of Christ, and shall dwell with him eternally in the heavens.

And the honor be to the Father, and to the Son, and to the Holy Ghost, which is one God. Amen.

This testimony was signed by Oliver Cowdery, David Whitmer, and Martin Harris.

Of these eleven witnesses, six left the Church, and of these six two returned to the organization. Not one of them, however, ever hinted a denial of his testimony of the divine origin of the *Book of Mormon*. On the contrary, every one of them affirmed his testimony to the last. This statement applies equally to those whose testimony involved the miraculous element and to those who saw only the plates.

Perhaps mention should be made here of the fact that many men and women of intelligence and substantial character accepted whole-heartedly the claims of Joseph Smith, as testified to by these

eleven witnesses. Among these were such men as
Brigham Young, Parley P. and Orson Pratt, Edward
Partridge, Newel K. Whitney, John Taylor, Wilford
Woodruff, Heber C. Kimball, Dr. Frederick G.
Williams, Dr. Willard Richards, and Orson Spencer
—all of whom knew intimately not only Joseph
Smith, but the witnesses as well. It would be hard,
one imagines, to deceive these men, with their in-
sight into character and their independence of spirit.

Since the publication of the *Book of Mormon*
considerable other evidence has been gathered to
prove its authenticity. Two lines of research may
be mentioned here.

The first deals with what is called external evidence. The book, during the hundred years and
more that it has been before the public, has been
strongly criticized because of its statements concerning the civilization of early America. That any culture of a high order existed in the Americas prior
to the coming of Columbus was generally doubted
at the time of the book's publication. Since then,
however, archeological research has confirmed the
record in many respects with proof of once populous
cities, of highly organized social systems, and of
destructive wars that destroyed great numbers of
people.

Another line of study lies in what is called in-
ternal evidence. This deals with the doctrinal unity
of the book, its consistency of language, its general
harmony, and Joseph Smith's inability to compose
such a work without divine help.

Chapter V

THE CHURCH IS ORGANIZED

All that Joseph Smith had accomplished thus far, and it was an extremely important work, was but preliminary to something even more important that was to come. An examination of the first religious experience of the Prophet and those other experiences involved in the coming forth of the *Book of Mormon* will show how preparatory these events really were.

In the First Vision he had learned (1) that God was verily a person, in whose image man had been created; (2) that Jesus Christ, who had been put to death in Palestine, was truly alive and had risen from the dead; (3) that God was willing to "give liberally" of his wisdom and knowledge to those who would ask him in faith; (4) that there is real efficacy in prayer; and (5) that the Church of Christ was not then on the earth, but that it would be restored through him under divine guidance.

In the visions relating to the *Book of Mormon* and in the labor of translating the ancient record, Joseph Smith had obtained a clear and broad view of theology and religion. The fact that God would be so concerned over the fortunes of ancient America was illuminating and helpful in itself. In showing the universality of God's love for mankind, the Nephite history threw a beautiful spotlight on the character of Deity. Also, as already suggested, the *Book of Mormon* is a treatise on theology and religion as well as a history. Its explanations of Christian doctrines are simple and clear. In the slow process of translation the Prophet, at an age when the learning process is very high, gradually absorbed the teachings set forth in the book.

Joseph Smith was in training for nearly ten years, as definitely as is a student in a law or a medical institution. Only in the Prophet's case, his tutors were God and Christ and Moroni. He needed training and discipline. He was young, he was inexperienced, he had small information, and the atmosphere in which he lived abounded in error. The work he was destined to do being God's work, his tutors must needs be divinely appointed, not to say heavenly beings. Time, too, was essential to perfect the education of the young man. Ten years, nearly, elapsed from the day of the First Vision to the completion of the translation. During most of this time he was under the direct tutorship of Moroni. The four years between the first revelation of the ancient record and the delivery of the plates to him, trained him to think of life in terms of service rather than of money, and at the same time turned his thoughts in the direction of God's purposes, not his own. That all this knowledge and training was effective is shown by the Prophet's subsequent career.

But this did not, however, give him the right to set up a church. The necessary divine authority was bestowed on the Prophet and Oliver Cowdery eleven months prior to the organization of the Church.

* * * * *

The account of the restoration of what is called the Aaronic priesthood is given thus by the Prophet:

We still continued the work of translation, when, in the ensuing month (May, 1829), we on a certain day went into the woods to pray and inquire of the Lord respecting baptism for the remission of sins, that we found mentioned in the translation of the plates. While we were thus employed, praying and calling upon the Lord, a messenger from heaven descended in a cloud of light, and having laid his hands upon us, he ordained us, saying:

"Upon you my fellow servants, in the name of Messiah, I confer the priesthood of Aaron, which holds the keys of the ministering of angels, and of the gospel of repentance, and of baptism by immersion for the remission of sins. . . ."

He said this Aaronic priesthood had not the power of laying on hands for the gift of the Holy Ghost, but that this should be conferred upon us hereafter; and he commanded us to go and be baptized, and gave us directions that I should baptize Oliver Cowdery, and afterwards that he should baptize me. Accordingly we went and were baptized, after which I laid my hands upon his head and ordained him to the Aaronic priesthood, and afterwards he laid his hands on me and ordained me to the same priesthood—for so we were commanded.

The messenger who visited us on this occasion and conferred this priesthood upon us, said that his name was John, the same that is called John the Baptist in the New Testament, and that he acted under the direction of Peter, James, and John, who held the keys of the priesthood of Melchizedek, which priesthood, he said, would in due time be conferred on us, and that I should be called the first elder of the Church and Oliver Cowdery the second.

It was on the 15th day of May, 1829, that we were ordained under the hand of this messenger, and baptized.

This statement by Joseph Smith is confirmed by Oliver Cowdery, with additional details.

Some time after this heavenly manifestation, the ancient apostles Peter and James and John appeared to the Prophet and Oliver, "in the wilderness between Harmony, Susquehanna county, and Colesville, Broome county, on the Susquehanna river." They declared themselves on this occasion to be in possession of "the keys of the kingdom, and of the dispensation of the fulness of times." Laying their hands on the heads of the two young men, they "ordained and confirmed" them "to be apostles and special witnesses" of Christ. This higher priesthood gave them authority to establish the Church on earth, with all that belongs to it by way of gifts, ordinances, and divine blessing.

On April 6, 1830, the Church was organized at the home of Peter Whitmer, in Fayette, New York. The following six men were the charter members of the organization: Joseph Smith, Jun., Oliver Cowdery, Hyrum Smith, Peter Whitmer, Jun., Samuel H.

Smith, and David Whitmer. They were all young men. Hyrum Smith, the oldest,· had just turned thirty, and Peter Whitmer, Jun., the youngest, was nearer nineteen than twenty. David Whitmer was twenty-five; Joseph Smith, twenty-four;.Oliver Cowdery, twenty-three; and Samuel H. Smith, twenty-two. All of them were farmers, except Oliver Cowdery, who was a school teacher.

The ceremonies connected with the organization of the Church were simple. The meeting was opened with "solemn prayer." Then the Prophet asked the men present whether they were willing to accept him and Oliver Cowdery as their, spiritual head. An affirmative vote resulted. After that the Prophet ordained Oliver Cowdery an elder and received ordination to the same office by Oliver. When the, six had been confirmed members of the Church (all of them had been baptized by immersion already), the Sacrament of the Lord's Supper was administered. Finally, the priesthood of elder was conferred upon others present.

Before the services adjourned Joseph Smith received a revelation, in which he was designated "a seer, a prophet, an apostle of Jesus Christ." This phrase is still continued in connection with the offices of the presidency, twelve apostles and presiding patriarch of the Church. As a forerunner of great things to come, the Holy Ghost, the account says, was poured out upon the new members "in great degree."

The name of the new organization was "The Church of Jesus Christ of Latter-day Saints." This is the official title of the organization. It is a significant name. On the one side the Church belongs to God, who is its creator; on the other, to the Saints in modern times. And then, too, the phrase "of Latter-day Saints" distinguishes it from the Saints in former days. Also, it is the Church of Jesus Christ as distinguished from that of some particular

man—Joseph Smith, for instance. Just as the followers of Jesus in the first years of our era were
nicknamed "Christians," so in this age his followers
have been nicknamed "Mormons," in allusion to the
Book of Mormon. Nevertheless, the true name of
the Church is that given it by revelation.

*   *   *   *   *

Very naturally this first organization was extremely simple. The only officers, as we have seen,
were a "first elder," Joseph Smith, and a "second
elder," Oliver Cowdery, who was also clerk and
kept the records. Its main principles and ordinances
were: (1) Faith, (2) repentance, (3) baptism, (4)
confirmation, (5) ordination, (6) the Sacrament of
the Lord's Supper. At first wine was used in the
sacrament, but presently water was served in this
rite on the ground that "it mattereth not what ye
shall eat and what ye shall drink when ye partake
of the sacrament, if it so be that ye do it with an
eye single to my glory." The foundation of all this,
of course, was the priesthood in its two degrees—
the Aaronic and the Melchizedek. The Latter-day
Saints first met for religious services in the home of
Peter Whitmer, in Fayette until a little later when
other homes were opened to them—Joseph Smith,
Senior's, in Manchester and in Fayette, and Joseph
Knight's in Colesville.

As the movement spread, however, the organization took on a more complex nature. In the revelation authorizing the creation of the Church, which
was received by the Prophet early in April, 1830,
the lesser, or Aaronic priesthood was divided into
three degrees—priests, teachers, and deacons. This
is the first mention of these offices, and in the revelation just referred to the duties of these officers
are outlined in some detail. All the officers of the
higher, or Melchizedek priesthood were called by
the name of "elder." In September, 1832, the office
of "high priest" appears, then, in February, 1835,

that of "seventy." Hence the Melchizedek priesthood, like the Aaronic, had three distinct offices,
although all those who held this higher priesthood
in any of its degrees were called by the general
term "elder."

In March, 1833, there appeared in the Church
what has since been known as the First Presidency,
although as early as January, 1832, Joseph Smith
was sustained as President of the High Priesthood.
His two counselors were Sidney Rigdon and Frederick G. Williams. In 1833 Joseph Smith, Sen.,
father of the Prophet, was set apart as a patriarch
—the first in the Church. His duty was to give
patriarchal blessings to members of the Church who
might come to him for this purpose. And in February, 1835, twelve apostles were chosen and the
first quorum of seventy. These offices correspond
with those in the primitive church.

The first quorum of the Twelve comprised the
following: Thomas B. Marsh, David W. Patten,
Brigham Young, Heber C. Kimball, Orson Hyde,
William E. McLellin, Parley P. Pratt, Luke S. John-
son, William Smith, Orson Pratt, John F. Boynton,
Lyman E. Johnson. This arrangement was accord-
ing to the age of the members, the oldest coming
first. The first presidents of the Seventy in the
Church were: Joseph Young, Levi W. Hancock,
James Foster, Daniel S. Miles, Josiah Butterfield,
Salmon Gee, and John Gaylord.

*   *   *   *   *

In an incredibly short time the movement extended into all the states of the Union and into Upper
Canada. Mormonism spread out over the country
because each member, as soon as he received baptism and ordination to the priesthood, felt it incum-
bent upon himself to go out and preach the gospel.
Said a revelation on the subject: "Verily I say unto
you, those who desire, in meekness, to warn sinners
to repentance, let them be ordained unto this power.

For this is a day of warning, and not a day of many words." And again: "It becometh every man who hath been warned to warn his neighbor. Therefore, they are left without excuse, and their sins are upon their own heads."

Perhaps the first missionary in the Church, after the Prophet himself, was his brother Samuel. Samuel, as soon as the *Book of Mormon* was issued, went into another county, his knapsack filled with copies of the book, partly to sell it but partly also to preach. Wherever he could not sell a book, he presented a copy to inquirers, either as a gift or as a loan.

Orson Pratt, after he had been baptized and ordained an elder, went out preaching in the country around Fayette—with what success we are not informed. He had been converted by his brother Parley P. Pratt, who had come to Palmyra after having read a copy of the *Book of Mormon*. Both Parley and Orson were natives of New York State.

The Prophet, with Oliver Cowdery and one or two others, preached in Colesville, presumably at the home of his old friend, Joseph Knight. He was successful in converting a number of men and women there, including the Knight family. For this activity, however, Joseph was twice arrested for disturbing the peace and twice acquitted in court. The neighbors of the Knights became not only abusive, but violent, toward the Prophet. He was imprisoned, he was brutally mistreated by those who guarded him, his witnesses were browbeaten; yet no offense against the law could be proved against him. This persecution, Joseph says, was instigated by preachers of the gospel, whose influence with their congregations was on the wane.

In spite of opposition, however, more than a hundred persons joined the Church in New York between April, 1830, and the spring of 1831. Besides the Smiths, the Whitmers, and the Knights, there were such families as the Rockwells, the Coltrins, and the Grovers, and Martin Harris. Some of these converts, like Martin Harris, Joseph Knight, and Thomas Grover, were well-to-do.. The first named, as we already know, furnished the funds with which the *Book of Mormon* was published, and the last named, on joining the Church, made the Prophet a gift of a considerable sum of money.

Chapter VI

THE CHURCH MOVES WESTWARD

As we have seen, one of the purposes in bringing forth the *Book of Mormon* was to reveal to the American Indians the life and character and teachings of their ancestors and to "bring them to Christ." No sooner, therefore, had the book been published and the Church organized than leading men in the Church began to think of the American Indians, of whose ancestors the Nephite record speaks. Had the time come, they asked, for these benighted people to receive the gospel?

In answer to an inquiry by "several of the elders" as to the "remnants of the House of Israel," Joseph Smith received a revelation calling Parley P. Pratt and Ziba Peterson on a mission "into the wilderness among the Lamanites." Oliver Cowdery and Peter Whitmer, Jun., had already been called to the same mission.

The women of the Church, headed by Emma Smith, prepared the things necessary for the journey —which was not an easy task, says Mother Smith, because "most of the necessary clothing had to be manufactured out of raw material." That was done, however, and in October, 1830, the men set out.

From Fayette, New York, to Northern Ohio— that was the first phase of their journey. Their reason for going to that place it seems, was that Elder Pratt had many friends there. Perhaps the most important of these was a minister named Sidney Rigdon—a preacher in the Church of the Disciples (Campbellite.) The pastor entertained the missionaries hospitably, but would not argue with them over the merits of their new faith. However, he promised to read the *Book of Mormon* carefully;

also to permit them to preach to his congregation. In the end both Rigdon and his congregation embraced the new movement.

"At Kirtland", says Elder Pratt, "the people thronged us night and day, insomuch that we had no time for rest and retirement. Meetings were convened in different neighborhoods, and multitudes came together soliciting our attendance; while thousands flocked about us daily; some to be taught, some for curiosity, some to obey the gospel, and some to dispute or resist it."

In the two or three weeks that they remained in the vicinity of Kirtland, they baptized one hundred and twenty persons. Among these were Sidney Rigdon, who was to become a counselor in the First Presidency of the Church, John Corrill, who later became one of the bishopric in "Zion," and Dr. Frederick G. Williams, who also became a counselor to the President of the Church.

About fifty miles west of Kirtland the missionaries stopped over night at the home of a Mr. Simeon Carter, with whom, when they departed, they left a copy of the Nephite Record. Carter, after reading the book, went to Kirtland, where he was baptized, and, returning to his home town, baptized some sixty persons and organized them into a branch.

It is well to remember that one of the four missionaries to the Lamanites was Oliver Cowdery, and that Oliver Cowdery had seen the plates and the angel and heard the voice of the Lord. So he could speak from personal knowledge.

* * * * *

After organizing the converts in Kirtland into branches with presiding officers, the missionaries to the American Indians proceeded on their way to the "borders of the Lamanites."

Their journey from now on was more hazardous than they had been led to expect. It was in the dead of winter, and snow lay heavy on the ground.

Their route touched Sandusky and Cincinnati, in
Ohio, and St. Louis and St. Charles, in Missouri.
The last three hundred miles led them over a wild
and desolate prairie, trackless and without inhabitants, except for an occasional hunter, and visited
frequently by keen north winds. They traveled the
entire distance on foot, save for a few days' ride up
the Ohio, the mouth of which they found impassable.
For whole days together they made no fire, and
ate nothing but raw bacon and frozen bread. Frequently they waded waist-deep in snow; they were
wet through by the rains; nearly always they were
cold and worn out by the toils of the day. But they
trudged heroically on, feeling that they were engaged in the service of God.

For some reason Dr. Frederick G. Williams
had insisted on joining the party after his conversion
and baptism in Kirtland. Dr. Williams at this time
was forty-four years old, the oldest in the group.

Arrived at Independence, Jackson county, Missouri, their long-sought-for "borders by the Lamanites," the missionaries laid their plans. Two of their
number obtained employment in the village as
tailors, while Elders Cowdery and Pratt crossed the
line in quest of the Delawares. By the chief of these
Indians—an aged sachem of many tribes—they were
received with kindness, and to him they communi-
cated their message of good will. After some hesi-
tation he consented to call a council of his chief
men, that they might listen to what the white missionaries had to say.

Elder Cowdery addressed the meeting. He
told the chiefs of the *Book of Mormon* and its re-
lation to their ancestors, and he gave the sachem a
copy of the volume, with the advice to read it and
cherish its teachings. The sachem thanked the two
for their present to him, and directed them to Mr.
Pool, the Indian agent, for entertainment. Mr. Pool
treated the two missionaries well and gave them food

and lodgings, but he forbade them to preach to the
natives. So Elders Cowdery and Pratt returned to
Independence. Their mission, as they thought, was
thus abruptly ended. By this time it was the middle of February.

At a council it was decided to send Elder Pratt
back to Fayette, to report the results of their mission thus far. On reaching Kirtland, however,
Elder Pratt found, to his surprlise, that the headquarters of the Church had been moved to Ohio.

As a mission to the Amercan natives this expedition had apparently failed, since there had been
no conversions among them. But as an opening to
the establishment of the Church in the West it was
eminently successful.

One of the distinctive features of Mormonism
is what has come to be called the "gathering." Where-
ever converts were made, up until recent years, they
were advised to "gather" to a central place. The
first gathering point was Kirtland, Ohio; then it became Jackson county, Missouri, and later in the region
of Far West, in the same state; after that it was
Nauvoo, Illinois; and, finally, after the migration
to the West, in Utah. The first indication of this
idea of gathering came in the New York period of
the Church.

In December, 1830, Sidney Rigdon and Edward
Partridge visited Joseph Smith in Fayette. Rigdon,
as we know, had already joined the Church. Partridge,
it seems, had been converted, but had not yet been
baptized. A man "who would not lie for his right
arm," as a neighbor of his declared, Partridge had
come to see the Prophet and to inquire into Mormonism.
The truth is that he had been appointed to do so by
some hesitant men in Kirtland, where he was a merchant. The next day after his arrival in Fayette, Partridge was baptized by the Prophet. He and Rigdon
stayed in the New York village for some time, and

when they returned to their home they took Joseph
and his wife with them. It had been revealed to the
Prophet that from now on the destiny of the new
movement lay in the West. Some time in April, 1831,
the more than one hundred converts moved to the
vicinity of Kirtland.

In less than one year, therefore, the Church numbered well over two hundred persons—the New York
group, the Mentor and Kirtland group, and those
whom Carter had converted. Among them were some
substantial men—Thomas B. Marsh, Sidney Rigdon,
Edward Partridge, who was to become the first bishop,
Parley P. Pratt, Orson Pratt, John Corrill, and Dr.
Frederick G. Williams.

It was in February, 1831, that the Prophet and
Emma arrived in Kirtland. They made their home
for a time with a merchant named Newel K. Whitney,
one of the Cowdery-Pratt converts there. Whitney
afterwards became presiding bishop of the Church.

From now on the new movement spread rapidly
over the country, and people entered the Church by
the hundreds. Missionaries went everywhere, traveling in pairs without "purse or scrip." Particularly
was the movement popular in Ohio.

The converts in New York—those in Manchester,
in Fayette, and in Colesville—went directly to a little
town near Kirtland, named Thompson. Here they
were established under an economic order, to be explained presently. Not long afterwards, however,
they moved to Jackson county, Missouri, with other
Saints. During the first years of the 1830's, therefore, there were really two separate gathering points—
Kirtland and adjacent Ohio towns and the region
known as Jackson county, in Missouri.

At a conference of the Church, held June 3, 1831,
many of the elders were called to go to Missouri. The
elders were instructed to go two by two and to preach

everywhere they went.   In addition it was decided that the Colesville branch, located at Thompson, Ohio, should go to Zion, as Independence, Jackson county, Missouri, came to be called.   Toward the middle of June, therefore, those who had been appointed to this mission began their journey thither.   They arrived at their destination about the middle of July, to make a settlement there.

At a place called Kaw the Colesville Saints were located.   The first log for the first house there was laid by twelve men representing the twelve tribes of Israel.   Sidney Rigdon dedicated the land, and later the Prophet himself dedicated at Independence a site for a temple.   On the occasion of the dedication of the land for the gathering of the Saints, those present covenanted "to receive this land with thankful hearts," to "pledge themselves to keep the law of God" there, and to "see that others of their brethren keep the laws of God" in all the settlements of the Saints in Zion.

Most of those who had come to Zion remained there to make a settlement.   Others, including the Prophet, Sidney Rigdon, and other leading elders returned to Kirtland.   Thus the nucleus of two separate settlements was formed, a distance of a thousand miles apart.

Chapter VII

EVENTS IN KIRTLAND

For a period of about seven years—from 1831 to 1838—we shall consider alternately the settlements in Kirtland, Ohio and Zion, in Missouri. This chapter will concern itself with events in the Ohio town; the chapter to follow, with events in the western settlement of the Saints.

During these years, years of great activity, the headquarters of the Church were in Kirtland, where the Prophet made his home. Every measure involving the new movement at any point began here. Missionary trips on anyone's part, the construction of houses of worship, the publication of tracts, books, and periodicals, the formation of business enterprises under the auspices of the Church, the planning of towns and cities—all these found their origin and inspiration in the Ohio town.

*   *   *   *   *

Land purchases were made in Kirtland and vicinity, to the amount of eleven thousand dollars. Some of this land was in city lots, but much of it was in farm land. Here, as in later places where they settled, the Saints showed that they possessed the qualities of industry, thrift, and intelligence. Kirtland, therefore, suddenly developed initiative and public-spiritedness, which attracted not a little attention. And its population increased steadily, notwithstanding the heavy drain upon that population by reason of the emigration to the western colony.

It was at this time, as the reader may recall, that new organizations came into existence within the Church—the First Presidency, the Quorum of Twelve

Apostles, the Seventy with its seven presidents. This was the period, too, when the High Council was created. The High Council is a judicial body, primarily; for before it come those who have difficulties to settle. It comprises twelve men with two or three alternates.

Shortly after finishing the translation of the *Book of Mormon* the Prophet undertook a revision of the Hebrew scriptures. It was in this Kirtland period that he completed it to the point where it was almost ready for publication.

In the Nephite Record he learned that, in the course of innumerable translations of the Bible, many "plain and precious" things had been taken away from it. A revision under divine inspiration would replace these plain and precious things. Such a revision he began in Fayette, New York, Sidney Rigdon, acted as his scribe, as Oliver Cowdery had done in the case of the *Book of Mormon*. It was taken up again after the Church headquarters had been moved to Kirtland. It was in Hiram, however, that the work was resumed. The Prophet and Rigdon, with Emma, went to live with a family named Johnson, members of the Church. And here, in this quiet retreat, most of the work of the revision was done. This revision, however, was never completed, and so it has never been published by the authority of the Church.

While living here the Prophet and Rigdon were subjected to persecution at the hands of residents of Hiram. A group of men invaded the home of the Johnsons, forcibly took them out a considerable distance from the house, stripped them to the skin, covered their bodies with tar, and otherwise mistreated them, finally leaving them for dead. Rigdon was dragged by his feet, with his head on the ground. He was delirious for some time afterwards. The men tried to force some nitric acid down the Prophet's throat, but the bottle broke against his teeth. He and some friends spent the rest of the night removing the tar from his body. The next morning, however, it being Sunday, he preached, but made no reference to the brutal episode of the previous night, although a number of the mobbers were present. This whole outrage was instigated by some articles printed in the *Ohio Star* against Mormonism, and the mobbers had been led by a preacher.

Other literary projects were carried on during this Kirtland period. One was the assembling and publication of the major revelations which the Prophet had received thus far. The volume was called *The Book of Commandments*. It was to issue from the press of the *Evening and Morning Star*, a Mormon publication in Independence, Missouri. The book did not make its appearance at this time, however, because, in 1833, the press and the papers were destroyed by a mob, and the building in which these were housed was demolished.

But the efforts of the leaders of the Church were not to be frustrated by such opposition. For in 1835 a volume of revelations actually appeared, under the title *Doctrine and Covenants*. An explanation on the title page told its readers that these revelations had been "carefully selected and compiled by a committee," which consisted of Joseph Smith, Sidney Rigdon, and Frederick G. Williams. It was printed in Kirtland, Ohio, "by F. G. Williams & Co. for the Proprietors."

As in the case of the *Book of Mormon* there were "witnesses" to the truthfulness of these revelations— the Twelve Apostles, who testified that "the Lord has borne record to our souls, through the Holy Ghost shed forth upon us, that these commandments were given by the inspiration of God, are profitable for all men, and are verily true."

In July, 1835, a man by the name of Michael H.

Chandler visited Kirtland. He had in his possession
rolls of papyrus, with characters on them. These
he was anxious to have translated. Having heard of
the Prophet and his work on the gold plates, Chandler
had come to see him, with a view of having him
give an opinion of them. Joseph translated some of
the characters, and the rendering of these, Chandler
said, agreed with that which some scholars had made.
Chandler was induced to sell these rolls of papyrus to
some of the Mormons in Kirtland. On closer examination they proved to be writings of Abraham, the
ancient patriarch. The Prophet at once began a translation of this roll. Owing however, to the troubles
he and his people endured in the two centers of Mormon population the manuscript did not appear in
printed form until after the Saints had moved to
Illinois. It was called the *Book of Abraham,* and is
now part of one of the standard works of the Church;
it is published in what is called the *Pearl of Great
Price.*

* * * * *

This literary undertaking brought about some
important advances in doctrine. Revelations which
the Prophet received during this period, many of
them growing out of his literary endeavors, gave new
light on human life and salvation.

For one thing, there is what is known among
the Latter-day Saints as the "Word of Wisdom." This
is a code which deals with the care of the body, with
a view of making it a fit abode of the human spirit.
Certain things are prohibited—hot drinks, including
tea and coffee, alcoholic stimulants, tobacco, and the
excessive eating of flesh. Others are enjoined—fruits
and vegetables "in the season thereof." And there is
a promise attached to the observance of these rules—
health, wisdom and long life. This revelation was

given in February, 1833, decades ahead of modern dietary science.

Two months before this, namely, in December, 1832, Joseph Smith received what is known among the Mormons as "A Prophecy on War." It is a singular document. The revelation predicts a war between the North and the South, in the United States, over the question of slavery,—the war was to begin in South Carolina, and eventuate in "the death and misery of many souls." Another detail specifies that the "Southern States will call on other nations, even the nation of Great Britain, in order to defend themselves." Another clause in this remarkable document states that "war shall be poured out upon all nations." Any one acquainted with United States history will recognize how every detail of this revelation, so far as the time has permitted, was fulfilled. It will be remembered too, that the problem of slavery had not then become a public question in the United States.

In this same period in Church history new light was received on the Other Life. The revelation on this subject was in the nature of an open vision to Joseph Smith and Sidney Rigdon. According to this vision there are three glories in the next life—the celestial, the terrestrial, and the telestial. And people are placed in these degrees of life in the hereafter on the basis of their "deeds in the flesh." All men are "saved;" that is, raised from the dead. But only those who have embraced the truths of the gospel are "exalted."

* * * * *

In December, 1832, the Prophet received a revelation instructing the Saints to build a "house of God." This was to be the first of nine temples erected to date by the Church. The particular purposes for which they are dedicated will be discussed later.

Notwithstanding the extreme poverty of the people a building committee was immediately organized and a call issued for means and workers. The cornerstones were laid July 23, 1833, the very day on which a Missouri mob demanded the removal of the

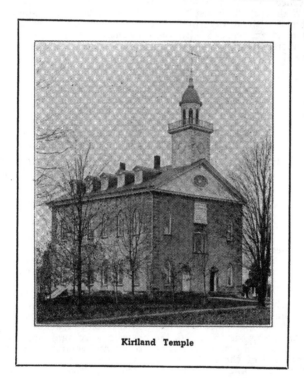

Kirtland Temple

Saints from Jackson county, as we shall see later. But in spite of these Missouri persecutions work on the temple continued without interruption. In describing the project Eliza R. Snow wrote:

At that time (1833) the Saints were few in number, and most of them very poor; and had it not been for the assurance that God had spoken, and had commanded that a house should be built to His name, of which He not only revealed the form, but also designated the dimensions, an attempt towards building that Temple, under the then existing circumstances, would have been, by all concerned, pronounced preposterous.

With very little capital except brain, bone and sinew, combined with unwavering trust in God, men, women, and even children, worked with their might. While the brethren labored in their departments, the sisters were actively engaged in boarding and clothing workmen not otherwise provided for—all living as abstemiously as possible, so that every cent might be appropriated to the grand object, while their energies were stimulated by the prospect of participating in the blessing of a house built by the direction of the Most High and accepted by Him.

The building was dedicated March 27, 1836. On the following Sunday, April 3, 1836, another meeting was convened in the building. After the administration of the Lord's Supper the Prophet and Oliver Cowdery retired to an enclosed portion of the hall. Here, abbreviated, are the Prophet's words on what took place.

> The veil was taken from our minds, and the eyes of our understanding were opened.
>
> We saw the Lord standing upon the breast-work of the pulpit, before us, and under his feet was a paved work of pure gold in color like amber.
>
> His eyes were as a flame of fire, the hair of his head was white like the pure snow, his countenance shone above the brightness of the sun, and his voice was as the sound of the rushing of great waters, even the voice of Jehovah...
>
> After this vision closed, the heavens were again opened unto us, and Moses appeared before us, and committed unto us the keys of the gathering of Israel from the four parts of the earth, and the leading of the ten tribes from the land of the north.
>
> After this, Elias appeared, and committed the dispensation of the gospel of Abraham, saying, that in us, and our seed, all generations after us should be blessed.
>
> After this vision had closed, another great and glorious vision burst upon us, for Elijah the prophet, who was taken to heaven without tasting death, stood before us and said:

Behold, the time has fully come, which was spoken of by the mouth of Malachi, testifying that he (Elijah) should be sent before the great and dreadful day of the Lord come,

To turn the hearts of the fathers to the children, and the children to the fathers, lest the whole earth be smitten with a curse.

Therefore the keys of this dispensation are committed into your hands, and by this ye may know that the great and dreadful day of the Lord is near, even at the doors.

* * * * *

It was in this period, also, that two important missions were undertaken by the Church.

Mormonism from the very first was a missionary organization. This was necessarily so. It was a new dispensation that Joseph Smith opened. Since mankind can be saved and exalted only through obedience to the gospel, of which the Church is the outward form and expression, it was imperative that men and women everywhere be given an opportunity to hear, and embrace or reject, the new revelation. And so nearly every one who held any degree of priesthood in the Church, became a missionary. At first no one waited to be called, but went out on his own responsibility.

At a conference of the Church, held in Kirtland in June, 1831, a call for missionaries was issued. This was the conference at which the first high priests were ordained. Many of the elders were asked to take missions to the West and preach by the way. From this time on, therefore, missionary work gradually developed into a system by which men were appointed to work for a more or less definite time in certain parts of the United States.

In 1836 the apostle, Parley P. Pratt, was appointed to a mission in Canada. His brother first and then the Prophet and Sidney Rigdon had been there, and had performed some baptisms. Elder Pratt at first met with only rebuffs in Toronto. But later he was invited to address a society of ministers, who met regularly to discuss the different Christian faiths and who were gradually coming to the belief that all of them had departed from the way. After three discourses Elder Pratt baptized all but one of this group of intellectuals.

From Toronto the work spread into other parts of Canada. Other missionaries were sent there from Kirtland to aid Elder Pratt. Among these were Orson Hyde, an apostle, and John E. Page, who later became an apostle. Elder Page alone baptized six hundred persons.

Some time later than this in the year 1837, Heber C. Kimball, one of the apostles, with Orson Hyde and Dr. Willard Richards, went to England on a mission. Four Canadian converts sailed with these missionaries from New York. One of the latter was Joseph Fielding, whose brother was a clergyman in Preston, England. On the way to New York City, Elders Kimball and Richards had stopped to collect some money due the latter for professional medical services. This lasted the two, however, only till they reached their destination; for when they landed, neither of them had a penny. A divine prompting led Elder Kimball to take his group to Preston.

In Preston they met the Reverend Mr. Fielding, who invited them to preach in his chapel. They did so and converted many of his congregation. Thus an opening was made in England. Presently the missionaries divided, in order to reach more people. The two apostles, with Joseph Fielding, stayed in Preston and preached. Not in Mr. Fielding's chapel, however, for that was closed to them when it appeared that the congregation was taking too much interest in the message of the Americans.

From now on baptisms were an almost daily occurrence. Elder Kimball on some days went into the water many times to perform the ordinance. And on each occasion he baptized from five to twenty-five persons. After eight months Elders Kimball and Hyde returned to America, leaving Elder Richards in charge.

River Ribble, Preston, England
-
Scene of First Mormon Baptism
In England

In this same year, too, Wilford Woodruff had a notable missionary experience. Having been ordained a priest, in 1834, he went on a mission to the Southern States. There he met with inconsiderable success. But later, when he had been ordained to the higher priesthood, he took a mision to the Fox Islands, off the coast of Maine. It was Sunday when he and his companion landed on one of the islands, and church was in progress five miles away.

"Tell the minister," he said to the deacon, when they reached the place, "that there are two servants of God at the door and that we have a message to deliver to this people."

The deacon did so, and the preacher invited them

to the front. A meeting was called for that evening, at which the newcomers preached. After sixteen meetings the missionaries converted all the people on the island, except the minister. They did the same thing on the other island. Before they left for home, they established two flourishing branches of the Church there, they had acquired for the Church two houses of worship, wholly paid for, and the two ministers were left without congregations.

This will give the reader an idea of how Mormonism spread in the United States, Canada, and England.

Chapter VIII

EVENTS IN MISSOURI

Meantime important events were rapidly taking place in the Mormon settlements in Jackson county, Missouri.

The first colony by the Latter-day Saints was established there, as the reader may recall, in August, 1831, sixteen months after the organization of the Church. The land was dedicated, a temple site was located, and the first houses built in Kaw township. And from then on an almost continuous stream of immigrants moved into the county in the covered wagon of the period. By the autumn of 1833 about twelve hundred Mormons had gone there to make their homes.

These settlers had every reason to be happy, despite the hard conditions under which they were living. They were industrious, thrifty, and intelligent, with a love for the beautiful. They were not typical frontier people. All of them had come from settlements that had been established from at least twenty-five to fifty years, in both Canada and the United States. And this land had a special significance to them. It was their Promised Land in a special sense. Here was to be built a city, planned for human welfare rather than for commercial purposes. Here, too, was to be erected a sacred temple. And so the Mormon settlers in the county went to work making improvements—building, plowing, planting, and harvesting, in the confident hope of making here a permanent home for themselves and their posterity. By the end of the year 1833 there were ten different settlements, the main one being at Independence.

Facilities for spiritual and intellectual development were set up in the Mormon community in Jackson county. The Saints carried with them their ideals of life and of thought. For one thing, they established a periodical. It was called *The Evening and Morning Star,* in allusion to their new-found faith. Its editor was William W. Phelps, who had had, besides a good education, not a little newspaper experience in New York. He was assisted by Oliver Cowdery. Independence being the prospective headquarters of the Church, the Saints were seeing to it that they were properly represented by the press. They owned and operated the plant from which issued the *Star.* It was here, too, that the *Book of Covenants* was to be published, and such other books as might be needed.

In addition, a "school of the prophets" was organized. This was for the benefit of the adult brethren. Here theology and religion were the chief study. It was a duplicate of a school established in Kirtland. But such secular subjects as English grammar, history, and geography were also in the curriculum. Had there been a competent teacher of the subject, Hebrew also would have been on the list, as was the case in the Kirtland school. The main purpose of this institution was to prepare the men for such missionary duties as they would certainly be called to perform.

*　*　*　*　*

Social-mindedness was perhaps the chief characteristic of the Saints in Jackson county. They had received this training under their prophet.

First of all, they had a unique civic community. The plan of the proposed city of Zion in Independence had been made under the direction of the Prophet himself. There had been nothing like it before. Its basis was not commercial, but social.

It was one mile square. The streets were eight rods in width and cut one another at right angles, so as to make what is called a gridiron, or chessboard, town. A public square was provided for, where the temple would be erected—a structure of surpassing beauty and stateliness. Each house, which would stand on a half-acre or less of ground, was set back on the lot far enough to provide for a lawn, with flowers, shrubbery, and ornamental trees in front, and for a garden in the rear. Every householder, therefore, was supposed to raise his own vegetables and fruit. The population of this town was not to exceed twenty thousand. Nineteen churches would take care of all the worshippers in the place.

On the outside of this town would be the farms, the factories, and the cemetery. Only shops were to be permitted within the city proper. Thus, as the Prophet stated, every man would live in the city. With the vegetables and fruit grown in the town and the cereals, the hay, and other large crops on the farms, and with such manufactured articles as the community required turned out in the mills and factories on the outside, each town would be almost self-sustaining. When this city was filled, as intended, other similiar cities would be built as needed. Smaller details of this civic plan were left to be worked out as conditions required.

A writer in the *New York Times*, himself a student of civic architecture, recently said of the Prophet's scheme that Joseph Smith was "far ahead of his time" in civic planning. In such a city there would be no places for slums, with their filth and degrading conditions, nor indeed for the apartment house, with its family of two or three. The whole aim of this plan was human welfare.

The economic structure of this model town was equally new and striking. Each householder would own his home and the land on which it stood, together with his implements of production, whatever they

might be. Here was, therefore, private ownership
and the incentives which go with it. But here private
ownership ceased, and public ownership began. Out
of his earnings every householder might take whatever was necessary for the maintenance of himself
and those dependent upon him. The rest, whether
large or small, he was required to turn over to the
bishop, as the representative of the community. In
this way the Prophet hoped to create a commonwealth
where there would be neither rich nor poor. It came
to be known as the United Order.

Whether or not this ideal would work was not
learned for certain, for the reason that, before it
could be put into practice long enough, the expulsion of
the Mormon people from Jackson county took place.
The idea was not taken up again by the Saints till
after the hegira from Illinois. Certain it is, however,
that Joseph Smith expected to supplant in the average
man the motive of love in the Christian sense for
the motive of selfishness as it is manifested in those
who have no religious restraints. And he hoped to
do this through a religion of *power* as contradistin-
guished from a religion of *form* merely.

* * * * *

At bottom it was this social ideal, saturated, as
it was, with the spirit of religion, that brought on a
clash of interests between the Mormons in Jackson
county and their neighbors. This ideal made the
Saints anti-slavery, because their religion laid such
stress upon the value of a human being—any human
being. The "old" settlers were strongly pro-slavery.
And it made them politically more or less unified,
since otherwise their ideal of economic life might be
jeopardized. There was a teamwork among them
which was totally lacking in their gentile neighbors,
who, being unrestrained frontiersmen, were emphatic-
ally individualistic. But the Missourian took partic-

ular affront at the belief of the Mormons, that this part of the West was their "inheritance," given them by the Lord.

Finally, there was what the Prophet often spoke of as the sleepless spirit of the "adversary of all righteousness." In its last analysis it was a contest between the forces of Good and the forces of Evil.

The conflict was not long in coming. Ever since the Mormons had been in the county, there had been rumblings of trouble. In 1832, some Mormon houses were stoned, haystacks burned, and meetings were held by the "old settlers" to see what might be done in the situation. And, in July, 1833, the gentiles drew up a "constitution," in which certain complaints were made against the new-comers and which demanded that the Mormons leave. There was not even a suggestion that the Saints had violated any law. On the contrary, the signers specifically declared that the "arm of the law" did not afford them protection "against the evils" which then afflicted them. The "constitution" was signed by several hundred persons, some of whom were officials.

Shortly after this the leaders of the two parties met and in the face of imminent hostilities drew up a "memorandum." In this document, which the Mormons signed under duress, it was agreed that all the Saints leave the county by the first of April, 1834. Considering that they had been forced to sign this "agreement," the Mormon leaders decided to appeal to the governor—which they did. This was after a mob had destroyed the press, books, and papers belonging to the "new" settlers, torn down the building in which they were housed and given a coat of tar on the public square to Bishop Partridge and Charles Allen. When, however, the Saints took steps to protect their rights by an appeal to the authorities, their enemies charged that the "agreement" had been broken. Thereupon they threatened to expel the Mormons from the county. In this critical situation John Corrill, John Whitmer, William W. Phelps, Algernon S. Gilbert, and Edward Partridge offered themselves as a ransom for the Church; they were willing to be put to death, if necessary, to appease the mob. But this sacrificial offer was without effect.

Then violence broke out afresh. On the night of October 31, 1833, some Mormon houses along the Big Blue river were unroofed, others were destroyed, and the inhabitants forced to flee for their lives. And on the night following a number of houses were demolished in Independence, and the store looted. Three days later a battle was fought between the gentiles and the Mormons on the Big Blue, in which two Mormons were killed. At this juncture the militia was called out ostensibly to protect the Saints, but really to drive them out of the county, for their first act was to disarm the Mormons. In the end, the Mormons were forced to leave. By November 7th the river banks were swarming with the refugees, who were without means of subsistence and shelter. Presently all of them found their way into Clay county, on the opposite side of the stream.

*   *   *   *   *

As soon as word reached Kirtland of what had happened to the Saints in Jackson county, steps were taken to relieve their distress and, if possible, to restore them to their homes.

In a revelation to the Prophet in December, 1833, he was required to gather together between one hundred fifty and five hundred "young and middle-aged men," and go "straightway into the land" which had been purchased by the Saints for an "inheritance." Accordingly, leading men in the Church, including the Prophet, went out into all the states seeking volunteers. They obtained more than two hundred men. This body was called "Zion's Camp." By the first of May, 1834, the camp was on its way to Missouri.

This group of men traveled without letting their identity or their purpose be known. Dressed in their ordinary clothes, they were not recognized as an army in the customary sense. But they aroused great curiosity everywhere. Their journey lay through Dayton, Indianapolis, Springfield, and Jacksonville. They reached Richmond, Missouri, June 19th.

Meantime, steps had been taken to bring about an amicable settlement of the difficulty. Negotiations were carried on with the leaders of the "old" settlers and with the governor. The Mormons refused to sell their land, and they were unable to meet the terms suggested by the opposition—to raise the money, probably half a million dollars, within thirty days. The governor said he would aid the Mormons to regain their homes, after which they could defend themselves—a proposal the Saints were willing to accept. This promise on the part of the governor, however, was not carried out.

Mormon losses in the expulsion from Jackson county ran around two hundred thousand dollars. Some of their property had been destroyed before their exile, but afterwards the houses that remained standing were set on fire. More than two hundred houses were thus destroyed. This was done, obviously, to deter the Saints from hoping ever to return.

A few of the Mormons had their faith shattered by these trials, but by far the greater number remained true. The new officers in the Church—the apostles and the presidents of the Seventy—were chosen from those who had proved faithful in the Camp of Zion.

Chapter IX

FURTHER EVENTS IN OHIO AND MISSOURI

When the Saints were driven out of Jackson county, they fled across the river into Clay county. They went there because there was nowhere else to go. And they were received by the settlers in Clay county with a humanity that contrasted with the brutality of the "old" settlers in Jackson county. This was due chiefly to a different sort of leadership in Clay county. We shall see presently how this eventuated.

In the main the Mormons hired out to the farmers there and took odd jobs as they could get them. Their expulsion from Jackson county having cost them about all they had in an earthly way, they had little or no property with which to start life anew.

As soon as it was made clear to the leaders of the Church that their people could not return to Jackson county and live there in peace, they looked around for a new home as close as possible to their beloved Zion. That is why they looked upon Clay county as only a temporary residence. Meanwhile, however, the gathering went on as before, pending the finding of a new home in Missouri. It was this gathering that made the settlers uneasy, lest they have the Mormons on their hands. This was so, particularly, because three years went by, and the Saints made no effort, apparently, to move. It was this anxiety, in part, that hastened the departure of the Mormons from Clay county.

Immediately to the north-east of Clay county was a wild and practically uninhabited prairie, whose wooded streams afforded haunts for droves of elk and

other wild game. At this time (1836) it was part of
Ray county, which had been created in 1820. Bee-
hunters and Indians were then almost the only human
beings to be found there. Nevertheless, it was one
of the most favored parts of upper Missouri, not only
for its fertile soil but also for its beauty. Bishop
Partridge and William W. Phelps had been over the
country, and recommended it for settlement by the
Saints. It had been suggested, also, by some leading
men in Clay county, who were anxious to get rid of the
Mormons.

In December, 1836, the county of Caldwell was
created by the legislature, and at the same time that
of Daviess just north of it, both out of Ray county.
While it was the intention to have the Mormons locate
in these two counties, there was no understanding that
gentiles were not to do so. Nor was there any agreement that the Mormons should not go elsewhere, if
they desired to do so. It was believed, however, that
the Saints would, for the present at least, confine
themselves to these two counties.

So the Mormons entered upon their task of homemaking with great energy and enthusiasm. It was
not long, therefore, till this section of upper Missouri,
under the well organized efforts of the Saints, assumed
an aspect of activity and progress that did not exist
in the older settlements in this part of the state. The
Saints established themselves at first on Shoal Creek
chiefly, a tributary of the Grand, but later they pushed
out into the different parts of Caldwell county. Ev-
entually they made settlements in Daviess county
and in Carroll county, just north of the Missouri, near
the junction of the Grand with this river.

The principal towns were Adam-ondi-Ahman,
in Daviess county, called Diahman for short, and Far
West, in Caldwell county. Adam-ondi-Ahman was
so called because "it is the place where Adam shall

come to visit his people." It is also the place "where Adam dwelt." Far West, with its surroundings, is declared in one of the revelations to be "a holy and consecrated land" unto God. It became not only the largest town in upper Missouri, but the county seat and the headquarters of the Church. It was located on Shoal Creek, northwest of what is now Kingston, the present county seat of Caldwell county. Here the Prophet and Sidney Rigdon came and made their home, when difficulties arose in Ohio.

In all perhaps fifteen thousand Latter-day Saints settled in this part of the state of Missouri. Dwelling houses were erected, schools established, farms cultivated, and the people generally looked forward hopefully to a prosperous and happy period.

* * * * *

Meanwhile in Kirtland things were fast coming to a climax for the Mormons.

In 1837 the Kirtland Safety Society Bank was established. Most of the leading men in the Church, including the Prophet, had stock in the institution, and some of them were officers. It was intended to aid the Saints in their financial undertakings. The officers bound themselves, in the articles of incorporation, to be responsible for the redemption of all notes given by the bank, proportionately to the amount of their stock. Prejudice against the Mormons, however, prevented them from obtaining a charter for the institution.

The bank failed. Several things contributed to its failure. First, it was not sanctioned by the state, and so other banks would not handle its paper. Second, one of its officers misappropriated its funds to the extent to twenty-five thousand dollars. This man later left the Church. Third, speculation was rife in Kirtland, as it was everywhere throughout the country. Fourth, in consequence of this speculation, values fell everywhere, including Kirtland, and banks failed in all parts of the United States. It would have been a miracle indeed if, under the circumstances, the bank had not failed.

Since, however, some leaders in the Church were originators of the bank and stockholders and officers in it, they were blamed for its failure. The Prophet in particular was criticized. Not a few men who had been prominent in the Church turned against the organization and its earthly founder. Among those who apostatized were the three witnesses to the divine origin of the *Book of Mormon,* some of the apostles, and one of President Smith's counselors. Most of these men, however, returned to the Church after they had had time to think. The three witnesses never at any time denied their testimony, but affirmed its truth everywhere, notwithstanding their apostasy from the organization. The disaffection spread into the ranks of the Missouri Saints and brought on apostasy there, too. It was a period of sorrow to the faithful. In the closing month of the year 1837 the Prophet and Sidney Rigdon went to Far West to make their home. In a little while all the Mormons in Kirtland left for Missouri.

* * * * *

One of the things done during this Far West period of the Church was to fill vacancies resulting from apostasy. This was not done all at once.

In the place of Frederick G. Williams, who lost his position of second counselor to President Smith in November, 1837, Hyrum Smith was chosen in the same month. Dr. Williams, however, moved to Missouri, was baptized again, and died a faithful member of the Church in Nauvoo, Illinois.

Changes were made also in the quorum of Apostles. John E. Page, John Taylor, Wilford Woodruff, and George A. Smith were set apart as members of this body, to take the places of William E. McLellin, Luke S. Johnson, John F. Boynton, and Lyman E. Johnson. Presently, however, Thomas B. Marsh turned away from the faith, though he afterwards returned, and David W. Patten was killed in a battle with a mob force. In their places were selected Willard Richards, who was then in England, and Lyman Wight.

It will be recalled that in 1831 the Law of Consecration was given for the benefit of the Church. This law was put into operation in Thompson, Ohio, and in Zion, Missouri. But it did not succeed, mainly because of the persecutions of the Saints in Jackson county. The law was never again attempted during the Prophet's lifetime. In this period, however, the law of Tithing was given in its place. Tithing requires only one-tenth of one's interest annually, whereas "consecration" demands all that one earns above what is necessary for the maintenance of oneself and dependents. Here is part of the revelation on tithing as revealed at this time:

> Verily, thus saith the Lord, I require all their surplus property to be put into the hands of the Bishop of my Church in Zion. . . . And this shall be the beginning of the tithing of my people. And after that, those who have thus been tithed shall pay one-tenth of all their interest annually; and this shall be a standing law unto them forever.

July 4, 1838, was a great day for the Saints in Missouri. There was a celebration in Far West, at which the Church leaders issued a declaration of independence from mobs. After the ceremonies the crowd assembled at the site for a new temple, excavations for which had been made before this, and the corner stones were laid. The building was to be one hundred and ten by eighty feet—larger than that in Kirtland, which was eighty by fifty feet.

But the troubles of the Saints were by no means

at an end. For, no sooner had they got settled in
their new home, than the enemy came once more upon
them. The story of this second expulsion is short.

Here is the chain of events leading up to that
expulsion: An election held in Gallatin, on August
6, 1838, resulted in a fight between the Mormons there
and the non-Mormons. The latter attempted to pre-
vent the former from casting their ballots. When
news of this affair reached Far West in an exaggerated form, some men armed themselves and went to
Gallatin to investigate. Joseph Smith was among the
number, although he did not carry a gun. Having.
obtained information as to the true situation, the men
returned to Far West. On their way, however, they
stopped at the home of Adam Black, a justice of the
peace and a non-Mormon, and obtained from him a
statement in writing of his peaceable intentions towards the Saints. It was dated August 8.

Just as the election contest had been exaggerated,
so now the incident of that journey into Daviess
county was made the most of by the leading gentiles.
For shortly afterwards an affidavit was signed by
several men, including Justice Black, who knew better,
to the effect that about five hundred Mormons, all
armed, had gone into Daviess county, for the purpose,
as they believed, of committing violence against the
non-Mormons. Of course, this provoked an uprising
on the part of the gentiles, who affected to believe that
they were in danger. This was the easier because
he who was lieutenant-governor at the time the Saints
were driven out of Jackson county—Lilburn W. Boggs
—was now governor. At first the opposition to the
Mormons was in the form of mobs, but later the mobbers were turned into the regular militia. The Mormons, too, armed to protect themselves. And so upper
Missouri became a war-infested area.

The contest was necessarily uneven. Battles were

fought, one of which was on Crooked river.   In
that battle the apostle David W. Patten and another
man were killed.   To make matters worse, Governor
Boggs issued an unwarranted and illegal order to drive
the Mormons out of the state or to exterminate them.
It is incredible that he should have done so, but he
did.   And this order was carried out to the letter.

Colonel George M. Hinckle, who had led a force
defending the Saints at Far West, capitulated to the
military authorities and agreed to surrender the Mormon leaders—all without Joseph Smith's knowledge.
Accordingly the Prophet, with Hyrum Smith, Sidney
Rigdon, Parley P. Pratt, and Lyman Wight, was arrested, tried by court martial, and sentenced to be shot
at sunrise on the public square in Far West.

This action on the part of Hinckle was a piece
of treachery to his people, since the imprisonment
of the leaders had been brought on through misrep-
resentation. And the trial of Joseph and Hyrum Smith
by court martial was illegal for the reason that
neither of them had carried arms nor advised any
insubordination to the state authorities. As a matter
of fact, Lyman Wight, who had led an armed force in
the field had done so to oppose a mob, acting on his
own authority.   It was only later in the difficulty that
these same men were taken into the militia.   And
then, too, as soon as it appeared that the Mormons
were fighting the militia, and on the request of the
leaders of the militia, the Mormon forces had given up
their arms.   The Saints had shown a disposition to
be peaceable, wishing only to protect themselves.

The Saints surrendered and gave up their arms,
and after being openly robbed by the militia, were
forced to leave the state.

Thus fifteen thousand American citizens were
compelled to abandon their homes in Missouri, and
this expulsion was carried on as winter was beginning

to set in. No consideration whatever was given the
Saints; no measures taken to protect their rights
to life or property. Their losses ran into a million
and a half dollars.

Chapter X

NAUVOO, THE BEAUTIFUL

Joseph Smith and his associates were not shot on the public square of Far West because General Doniphan, to whom the execution order was given, refused to carry it out. "It is cold blooded murder," he replied to Major General Lucas. "I will not obey your order. My brigade shall march for Liberty tomorrow morning, and if you execute these men, I will hold you responsible before an earthly tribunal, so help me God."

Nauvoo, The Beautiful

But all the prisoners were taken to Independence first and then to Richmond and Liberty, and kept in prison for nearly six months, with only a one-sided trial. Most of them escaped at last without resistance from the officers who guarded them. There was no evidence against the prisoners, and they could not be convicted.

During this imprisonment, the Prophet received many important revelations and gave some valuable instructions to his people. Among the ideas advanced by him at this time was that recorded in section 121

of the *Doctrine and Covenants,* that "no power or influence can be maintained by virtue of the priesthood, only by persuasion, by long-suffering, by gen-
tleness and meekness, and by love unfeigned."   It
was here, too, that he was given a hint that fore-
shadowed his martyrdom.   He told Lyman Wight
that he would never live to see his fortieth birthday,
but asked him not to tell anyone of this till after his
death.

The Prophet, with some of his prisoner-com-
panions, arrived in Quincy, Illinois, some time in April,
1839, and immediately set to work on a plan for re-
settling his people in that state.

*   *   *   *   *

Meantime many things had happened to the
Saints, both in Missouri and in Illinois.

General Clark, who had taken a prominent part
in bringing matters to a climax in Missouri, came to
Far West.   Here, under orders from General Lucas,
he placed all the men in Adam-ondi-Ahman under
arrest, and proceeded to appropriate what Mormon
property he could to defray the expenses of the militia in driving the Saints out of the state.   "You must
not think of staying here another season or of putting in crops," he told the Mormons, "for the moment
you do this, the citizens will be upon you.   If I am
called here again, . . . you need not expect any mercy,
but extermination."   He was acting, he said, for
General Lucas—the man who had ordered Joseph
and Hyrum Smith shot at Far West without a hearing.

There is every reason to believe that the expulsion of the Mormons from Missouri was a deep-laid
plot by the governor and other high officials in the
government.   And there is equal reason to believe
that the imprisonment of the Mormon leaders was
a part of that scheme, as was their "escape" from the
hands of the officers placed to guard them.

The Saints had been leaving Missouri as fast as they could do so. The destination of most of these refugees was Quincy, Illinois. This exodus of fifteen thousand men, women, and children occurred in the winter time. Necessarily it entailed much suffering on the part of the aged, the women, and the children. Mother Smith's experience was typical. Sister Smith was the mother of Joseph and Hyrum Smith. She says:

> The first day we arrived at a place called Tinney's Grove, where we lodged over night in an old log house, which was very uncomfortable. Half of the succeeding day I traveled on foot. That night we stayed at the house of one Mr. Thomas, who was then a member of the Church. On the third day, in the afternoon, it began to rain. At night we stopped at a house and asked permission to stay till morning. The man to whom we applied showed us a miserable out-house, which was filthy enough to sicken the stomach, and told us, if we would clean this place and haul our own wood and water, we might lodge there. To this we agreed, and, with much trouble, we succeeded in making a place for our beds. For the use of this loathsome hovel he charged us seventy-five cents.
>
> We traveled all the next day in a pouring rain. We asked for shelter at many places, but were refused. At last we came to a place quite like the other one where we spent the previous night. Here we spent the night without fire. On the fifth day, just before arriving at Palmyra, in Missouri, Don Carlos called to Mr. Smith, and said, "Father, this exposure is too bad, and I will not bear it any longer; the first place I come to that looks comfortable, I shall drive up and go into the house, and do you follow me. . . . "
>
> At this house (the next one they came to) we had everything which could induce to comfort. . . .
>
> After spending the night with this man we proceeded on our journey, although it continued raining, for we were obliged to travel through mud and rain to avoid being detained by high water. When we came within six miles of the Mississippi river, the weather grew colder, and, in place of rain, we had snow and hail; and the ground between us and the river was so low and swampy that a person on foot would sink in over his ankles at every step; yet we were all of us forced to walk, or rather wade, the whole six miles.

On reaching the Mississippi, we found that we could not cross that night, nor yet find shelter, for many Saints were there before us, waiting to go over into Quincy. The snow was now six inches deep, and still falling. We made our beds upon it, and went to rest with what comfort we might under such circumstances. The next morning our beds were covered with snow, and much of the bedding under which we lay was frozen. We rose and tried to light a fire, but, finding it impossible, we resigned ourselves to our comfortless situation.

About sunset we landed in Quincy. Here Samuel had hired a house, and we moved into it, with four other families.

Lucy Smith was sixty-two years old at this time, and her husband sixty-seven. He died about a year after this bitter experience, one of the many victims of persecution, on account of his religious faith.

In Illinois the exiles were received with a spirit that contrasted with that which they had found in the neighbor state. Leading citizens in Quincy got together and appointed a committee, whose duty it was to find work and suitable homes for the refugees. And this committee did a good service as long as it was in active operation. This was between the months of November, 1838, and April, 1839.

During these months, however, committees of the Mormons were at work. Some of these sought to co-operate with the Quincy committee in obtaining houses and employment for their people. Others were organized to find a suitable place for settlement, either in Illinois or Iowa. Hence, when the Prophet arrived in Quincy in April, 1839, after more than five months' imprisonment, all the Saints had left Missouri, most of them were settled temporarily in Illinois or Iowa, and their interests reasonably taken care of. Immediately, however, he began measures for their permanent location.

* * * * *

Up the Mississippi about fifty miles from Quincy

there was a place that went by the name of Commerce. It was situated in a graceful bend of the stream, on the eastern side, and sloped gently upward toward the prairie. Having been a landing place for boats plying up and down the river, there were still a few houses of lumber or of rock. These were near the bank. The ground, however, from lack of drainage, was so boggy that a man could scarcely make his way from one side to the other, and a team not at all. Here and there were some scrubby trees and bushes.

This place was chosen by the Prophet as the future home of his people, and in anticipation of a realization of what he had in mind, he called it Nauvoo, which means "beautiful." Land was bought from a Mr. White and a Dr. Galland in Commerce and vicinity, also on the west side of the river in Iowa. Dr. Galland had advised the Mormons to settle in Iowa, which was then a territory, because he thought they would be more likely to receive protection from the Federal government than if they settled in a state, "where," he said, "the greatest villians often reach the highest offices." Some of the Saints settled in Iowa, but the great body of people remained in Illinois. As soon as land purchases had been made, the Saints began to occupy Commerce and Montrose. Montrose was on the Iowa side of the river.

The first thing that happened to the people on both sides of the stream was a severe attack of the fever and ague. This was owing partly to the dampness of the ground, partly to the mosquitoes, and partly to the run-down condition of the Saints. Some were in houses there, but others were in tents, for there had not been time to build houses. The Prophet himself, who had turned over his home to the sick, was down with the fever. One morning, however, he rose from his sick bed and began administering to

the sick in the vicinity of his own home, and they
were immediately healed. Then, with a few of the
brethren, he went to others who were sick, and these
also were healed. After that he passed over to Montrose, Iowa and healed all who were sick there. Verily,
as Elder Wilford Woodruff, who relates the incident
in detail, tells us in his *Journal*, it was a day of God's
power. What might have become a calamitous event
was turned into a blessing.

At first it was apparently intended that the
Saints should occupy a large area in Illinois and Iowa,
but this idea was abandoned for a plan of concentration. Five stakes were organized to begin with,
but presently three of these were disorganized, which
left only one stake on each side of the river. (A
"stake" is a division of the Church which corre-
sponds to a diocese in some other Christian churches.)
In 1841, however, the Saints were required, in a
revelation, to gather in Hancock county, Illinois, and
in Lee county, Iowa. During the first year, therefore,
Nauvoo had a population of about six thousand, and
before long a population of between twenty and
twenty-five thousand. It became the largest town in
the state.

In December, 1840, Nauvoo was incorporated.
Its charter, which was granted by the legislature,
was probably the most liberal ever granted to any
American city. Really, under this charter, Nauvoo
became what is known as a "city state." Besides
the usual privileges given to towns, Nauvoo had an independent judiciary and an independent militia, with
a university. There was a mayor, with a council
composed of aldermen and councilmen. This body
had all the powers customarily granted to justices
of the peace, and sat in both civil and criminal cases.
The Nauvoo Legion, which numbered between four
and five thousand men, was independent of the state

militia, although it was subject to the call of the governor in any situation. The University of the City of Nauvoo was authorized to teach "the arts, the sciences, and the learned professions." Orson Spencer, who had a master's degree, was its chancellor, or president, and Orson Pratt, who was to become a celebrated mathematician, was a professor there. The first mayor was Dr. John C. Bennett, who had worked for the charter. He did not serve in this capacity for long, however, and Joseph Smith, who had conceived the charter, took his place.

One of the singular things about the government provided for this city was that it granted and guaranteed absolute freedom of religious worship, with penalties for disturbing the peace of any church. Here were the Mormons who had suffered violently at the hands of religious bigotry, nevertheless protecting all religions in a town for which they were wholly responsible.

Nauvoo soon presented a picture of industry, intelligence, thrift, and happiness. This is testified to by all who came to visit the city. At first the houses were of logs, many of them. This was because the people were poor, having been stripped of their property in Missouri. But houses of lumber, of brick, and of rock presently appeared. Some of these houses were in the best Colonial style—the best form of this style of architecture to be found in early Illinois. The streets were wide and ran from east to west and from north to south, according to the lines of the compass. And there were stores and shops, one of which was owned and operated by Joseph Smith. It was in the upper room of this store that the endowments setting forth the ancient order were instituted for the first time in this dispensation. Here, too, the Prophet instructed the men close to him in the "mysteries of the kingdom."

The spectacle of a people rising, phoenix-like, from the ashes aroused attention in those who could see the better aspects of life, social and individual. The Mormons could not be defeated in their purpose. They rose above every discouragement. And so Nauvoo was often thronged with visitors,. who had come from many places to see this miracle of courage, determination and progress.

Chapter XI

EVENTS IN THE NAUVOO PERIOD

One of the first things to be done by the Prophet, his people having been settled, was to seek redress for the wrongs suffered by the Mormons in Missouri. We have seen that, when the Saints were expelled from Jackson county in that state, their leader advised them to appeal to the governor for restitution and redress. They did this, but to no purpose. Now he proposed to appeal to the Federal government for redress on a more extensive scale.

Sidney Rigdon wanted to impeach Missouri for abandoning republican principles, and in this plan he was aided by the governors of Illinois and Iowa. The scheme, however, was too impractical to promise any degree of success. So, in April, 1839, Joseph Smith sent out an appeal to the citizens of the United States, in which he "invoked the genius of the Constitution." He called upon them to "rise up in their majesty" and "bring the offenders to that punishment which they so richly deserve." Nothing came of this appeal, so far as was evident in any action. In the following month President Rigdon was appointed to carry the message of the victims of persecution to Washington, and in October of this year (1839) President Joseph Smith and Judge Elias Higbee were added as members of a committee of three to visit Washington authorities. Martin Van Buren was then president.

In November President Smith and Judge Higbee called on President Van Buren. Elder Rigdon had been delayed on the way. The President's comment was a question—"What can I do? I can do nothing for you. If I do anything, I shall come in contact with the whole state of Missouri." On being pressed, however, Van Buren promised to consider the matter. Shortly afterwards the delegation had a petition presented to the Congress. The representatives advised that the Mormons appeal to the judiciary of Missouri—a proposal which the Prophet vigorously opposed, on the grounds of its utter futility. The Congress, however, did nothing in the matter, and ordered the committee dismissed. After another visit to the President, the Prophet returned to Nauvoo, arriving there in March, 1840.

The Saints had now done all in their power to carry out the command of the Lord, to "importune at the feet of the judge, at the feet of the governor, and at the feet of the president; and if the president heed them not, then will the Lord come forth out of his hiding place, and in his fury vex the nation." That "vexation" came to Missouri partly in the Civil War and after effects. For, according to Governor Robert M. Stewart, "This state has probably lost as much, in the last two years, in the abduction of slaves, as all the rest of the Southern States. At this moment (1861) several of the western counties are desolated, and almost depopulated, from fear of bandit hordes, who have been committing depredations—arson, theft, and foul murder—upon the adjacent border."

* * * * *

In this period missionary enterprise manifested itself in a marked way. Literally thousands were converted to Mormonism in the United States, in Canada, in England, and on the islands of the Pacific.

No sooner was a site chosen for the Saints than a call was issued for the Twelve to go to England. Indeed, this call was made before a resting place had been found for the feet of the Mormons. Most of the apostles left Nauvoo in the summer of 1839. One of the Twelve was already in England—Willard Richards—although he had not yet been ordained to that office. William Smith and John E. Page, though they left Nauvoo, did not go on the mission to which they had been called. The first to leave on this mission were Elders John Taylor and Wilford Woodruff. They started on July 8. Next Parley P. Pratt and Orson Pratt took their leave. Parley had just made his escape from a Missouri prison nineteen days before, aided by his brother Orson. These two were followed two months later by Elders Brigham Young and Heber C. Kimball, both of whom were recovering from sickness. And three days later Elder George A. Smith left Nauvoo, with two companions, all three of them sick. These men had left their families in the care of fellow members.

Orson Hyde and John E. Page had been called to go to Palestine. The latter, as already stated, had left Nauvoo, apparently on this mission, but he did not get farther than New York City. Elder Hyde went on alone. In October, 1841, he ascended the Mount of Olives and dedicated the land of Palestine for the gathering of the Jews. Here, too, and on Mount Moriah, he erected a pile of stones as a witness to what he had done. The mission was in fulfilment of a prophecy, made ten years before this, that he should "go to Jerusalem, the land of thy fathers, and be a watchman unto the House of Israel," and that he should do a work "which shall prepare the way and greatly facilitate the gathering of that people." It is not, therefore, a coincidence that shortly after the dedication of Palestine by Elder Hyde the Jews should begin to look toward that country and gather there. Today there are nearly three hundred thousand Jews in the Holy Land, under the protectorate of Great Britain. Circumstances have been shaping to almost force the gathering of Israel to that land.

Eight of the apostles labored in Great Britain. This included Elder Richards, who was ordained one of the Twelve in England. At this time there were thirty-four branches of the Church there, with one hundred twenty-eight men holding the priesthood— all converts to the faith. The total membership was sixteen hundred eighty-six. At a conference of the Saints in the British Isles, held in April, 1840, it was decided to publish a periodical, to be called *The Millennial Star* and a hymn book for the use of the churches. And presently a copyright was obtained for the *Book of Mormon,* an edition of which was issued in England.

Marked success followed the preaching of the gospel there. This was particularly so in the case of Elder Woodruff, who baptized eighteen hundred persons in Herefordshire alone. He had gone there in response to a divine revelation received while he was preaching in Hanley. A society calling itself the United Brethren had been organized in Herefordshire, in anticipation of the coming of the true church at an unknown future date. The organization numbered six hundred, with scores of preachers. All of these, with one exception, embraced Mormonism. The first one baptized by Elder Woodruff was John Benbow, a wealthy farmer, who contributed fifteen hundred dollars to publish the *Book of Mormon.*

Before the missionaries left England they had increased the membership of the Church to four thousand. During this time many manifestations of divine power occurred—healing the sick, casting out of evil spirits, speaking in tongues, and other miracles. Here is one case, related by Elder Woodruff: "Mary Pitt . . . had not walked for eleven years. We carried her into the water, and I baptized her. On the evening of the 18th of May, in 1840, at Brother Kington's house in Dymock, Elders Brigham Young, Willard Richards, and I laid hands upon her head and confirmed her. Brigham Young, being mouth, rebuked her lameness in the name of the Lord, and commanded her to arise and walk.

The lameness left her, and she never afterwards used a staff or crutch. She walked through the town of Dymock next day, and created a stir among the people thereby."

It was in this Nauvoo period of the Church, too, that light was thrown upon the idea of salvation and the purposes of the Lord.

In 1832 a revelation on the degrees of glory in the next world showed that heaven was not one stage but many stages. Light was thrown upon the phrase "many mansions," used in the Bible. The Prophet, as we have seen, had previously taught that certain requirements were necessary for the attainment of the highest degree of glory in the hereafter. But, until this period, the extent of God's plan of human redemption was not understood by the Saints. The phrase, so often used by them, "the plan of life and salvation," acquired a new meaning at this time.

God brought the earth into existence for the purpose of promoting the development of man. This growth was to come through adherence to the gospel, which includes every principle, individual and social, temporal and spiritual, that is necessary to insure happiness here and exaltation hereafter. But, in order to be happy through this means, man must first hear and then obey the principles of the gospel. But there have been long periods of time during which the gospel, through man's disobedience, has not been preached on earth. Besides, during the time when the gospel has been here, not all men have been fortunate enough to hear it. What is to become of those who, for either of these reasons, have not been privileged to embrace the gospel? The Christian world had no answer to this question. It will be seen, then, that God, according to the prevailing notion, had made a plan so imperfect as to miss the greater number

of his children. He was thus represented as either
unjust or inefficient.

The Prophet Joseph Smith, however, in the Nauvoo period had revealed to him the answer to this
perplexing question. It is called salvation for the
dead.

Man consists of two essential parts. One of these
is spirit; the other, flesh. The body is the abode of
the spirit. The spirit existed before it came here,
it exists here in the body, it goes at death into the
spirit world, and in the resurrection it will re-occupy
the body which it had in this life, in its essential
elements. It is the spirit, not the fleshy body, that
thinks, and wills, and feels. It is the spirit, not the
body, that accepts or rejects truth that is to "save"
it. This being so, the acceptance or the rejection of
gospel truth is not limited to earth. After death the
gospel may be heard and received; that is, in the
spirit world. However, certain ordinances are necessary, regardless of where one is before one can enter
the celestial kingdom. One of these is baptism by
immersion for the remission of sins by one having
divine authority. Another is confirmation, the imposition of hands for the reception of the Holy Ghost.
And still others are the ordination to priesthood
and marriage for eternity and time.

Now, these ordinances are of such a nature that
they can be performed only in the flesh. But those
spirits who accept the gospel in the world of spirits
have left the earth and the flesh. How, then, can they
be baptized, confirmed, receive priesthood, and be
sealed in marriage? The answer is, through the
baptism, the confirmation, the ordination, and the
sealing of some one else for them. The acceptance
of truth is in the spirit; the rites and ceremonies,
in the flesh. Thus all mankind will have the opportunity of receiving or rejecting the gospel, either in

the flesh or in the spirit. And thus, too, the responsibility is placed definitely on man. This idea of
salvation for the dead puts God in a new light. He
becomes a God of universal mercy and justice to all
men, both the living and the dead. Also it explains

Nauvoo Temple

the phrase, "baptized for the dead," used by Paul,
and the phrase, "preached to the spirits in prison,"
used by Peter.

At first baptisms for the dead were performed in
the Mississippi river, but as soon as it could be done,
they were performed in the temple, which was being

erected in Nauvoo. This temple was among the first
buildings planned in that city. The building was
begun in April, 1841. Every tenth day was to be de-
voted to work on it by the men who belonged to
the Church. The temple was one hundred twenty-
eight feet long, eighty-eight feet wide, and sixty-five
feet to the square. From the ground to the top of
the spire was one hundred sixty-five feet. The
material was light gray limestone, nearly as hard
as marble, though there was much wood in the building. There were thirty hewn pilasters—nine on each
side and six on each end—the capitals of which, at
a height of fifty feet, were suns with human faces
in bold relief two and a half feet broad, ornamented
with rays of light-waves, and surrounded with hands
holding trumpets. There were two stories in the
clear. On the west side of the building were inscribed
in gold the words, "The House of the Lord." The
total cost exceeded one million dollars.

The first baptisms in the temple were performed
in November, 1841, the baptismal font having been
completed and dedicated by this time. The temple,
however, was not finished till after the death of the
Prophet. Before the exodus of the Mormon people,
in the early spring of 1846, ordinances for the living
and baptisms for the dead had been performed within its sacred walls.

*   *   *   *   *

In March, 1842, the editor of the *Chicago Demo-
crat*, John Wentworth, requested the Prophet to submit to him an article on Mormonism. Wentworth
wished the article for a Mr. Barstow, who was writing
a history of New Hampshire. The article is of importance chiefly because it contains what has since
come to be known as the "Articles of Faith" of the
Church. These are remarkable for their simplicity,

conciseness, and comprehensiveness as statements of Church doctrine.

In the same month the first of the "auxiliaries" to the Church was organized—the Relief Society, a woman's organization. It was the first society of its kind, not only in America, but in the world. Its purpose is indicated in its title. The Relief Society now, however, has courses in literature and religion, as well as in social welfare.

Chapter XII

MARTYRDOM OF JOSEPH AND HYRUM SMITH

The Mormon people, as we have seen, were well received in Illinois. This reception was due, as we have also seen, to the fact that their distress went to the hearts of the citizens of Quincy. But the Saints had not been in the state very long till they began to be in difficulties again. And in this case it came about that their Prophet and Patriarch were murdered by a mob in Carthage.

* * * * *

In July, 1840, four Mormons were attacked by mobbers in Hancock county and taken across the border into Missouri. Presumably the attackers were from that state. They declared that they would kill every Mormon they could find. Two of the kidnapped were released a few days after their capture, but two others were kept in irons for more than a month, when they made their escape.

In September, 1840, the governor of Missouri issued a requisition on the governor of Illinois for Joseph Smith, Sidney Rigdon and four others as fugitives from justice. The requisition was granted by Governor Carlin. An attempt was made to capture the Prophet, who had gone to Springfield to interview the governor, to kidnap him and take him over the state line into Missouri. His enemies were not content to trust to the law. But this attempt was frustrated by Joseph's friends. The Prophet was released on a writ of habeas corpus, and tried before Judge Stephen A. Douglas. The decision was that the writ was "dead."

On May 6, 1842, Lilburn W. Boggs, who was

now out of office, was shot at his residence in Independence, Missouri. Immediately the Mormons were charged with the crime. Specifically it was charged to Orin Porter Rockwell as principal and Joseph Smith as accessory before the fact. The motive was presumed to be revenge. There followed another requisition from the governor of Missouri upon the governor of Illinois for Rockwell and the Prophet. Accordingly the two men were arrested on a warrant issued by Governor Carlin. The arresting officers, however, having no papers with them, the men were allowed their liberty. So both Joseph and Rockwell disappeared. The Prophet went into hiding, and Porter left the state.

Meantime, Thomas Ford succeeded Thomas Carlin as governor of Illinois. Meantime, too, friends of the Prophet were active in his behalf. They besought the new governor to declare void the requisition from Missouri. He refused on the ground that he had no authority to alter a decision made by his predecessor in office. So the matter went into the court. The prisoner was discharged. Rockwell, however, was arrested in Missouri and kept a prisoner there for about six months. An attempt was made to use him as a decoy for the kidnapping of the Prophet, but, to his credit, he refused to betray his friend, preferring to suffer himself.

* * * * *

Meantime enemies of the Prophet were arising in Nauvoo. It will be remembered that Dr. John C. Bennett had been made mayor of Nauvoo, chiefly as a reward for his services in getting the charter through the legislature. Bennett was a scoundrel at heart. He probably joined the Church to further his ambition for power. At any rate, he left the Church when he was caught in certain immoralities. This was in 1842. On leaving Nauvoo he published a book against his former friends, *The History of the Saints.* Besides, he associated with President Smith's enemies in Missouri, furnishing them with what in-spiration they lacked for further persecution of the Mormons. Moreover, Bennett, through letters he wrote to Sidney Rigdon and Orson Pratt, tried to implicate others in his scheme to destroy the Prophet. Elder Pratt promptly turned these communications over to President Smith.

As a result partly of Bennett's activities the Prophet was arrested near Dixon, Illinois, by two officers from Missouri and two from Illinois. This was in pursuance of a plan to take him across the border into Missouri. He was tried before the muni-cipal court in Nauvoo, and acquitted. Thus another attempt on his life was frustrated.

Other enemies there were in Nauvoo. Among these were the brothers William and Wilson Law, the brothers Francis M. and Chauncey L. Higbee, and the brothers Charles A. and Robert D. Foster. These combined with others to deprive the Prophet of the power which he exercised over his people. They had been handled by him for their fellowship. Their os-tensible reason was that President Smith had too much power. Towards June, 1844, these six men affil-iated with Joseph's enemies outside the city and with Dr. Bennett, who was in communication with enemies in Missouri.

Moreover, during most of the time the Saints were in Illinois there was a growing sentiment against them in Hancock county over politics. In self-protection the Mormon people usually voted to-gether, and this always turned the election in the county and sometimes in the state. Not always the same party won, of course, for the Saints cast their ballots for candidates who were their friends. This made the losers angry, who vented their spleen against the Mormons in general and Joseph Smith in particular. The result was an increasing antagonism.

In order to avoid political trouble as much as possible, the Saints put the Prophet forward as a presidential candidate, with Sidney Rigdon, who had moved to Pennsylvania, as vice president. This was in 1844. President Smith issued a pamphlet setting forth his views on government, which attracted considerable attention throughout the nation. In this pamphlet he advocated the purchase of all the slaves in the United States by the government and then freeing them, thus compensating their owners and at the same time liberating men and women from bondage. Another measure suggested in this pamphlet was that all offenders against the law be placed in schools rather than prisons, where they might be taught vocations and religion, so as to make them fit to re-enter society. This, as a matter of fact, is the tendency to-day, as seen in the juvenile courts in the United States. The Prophet also advocated national and state banks, to retain control of money in governmental hands. To make this independent candidate known, hundreds of men left Nauvoo and went electioneering, with the result that Joseph Smith became more favorably known throughout the nation.

* * * *

The Prophet's difficulties came to a climax in June, 1844. The occasion was the publication, on the tenth of this month, of a periodical called *The Nauvoo Expositor*. Its principal owners were the six men already named—the Laws, the Higbees, and the Fosters. The purpose of the sheet was to break down the power of Joseph Smith. It sought to have the charter revoked, and it attacked the motives and actions of Nauvoo's leading citizens.

The publication of the *Expositor* created a sensation in Nauvoo. Every one was outspoken in de-

nouncing it as a libel. Feelings were tense. The
city council met, took evidence, read the law on the
subject of nuisances, consulted the charter to ascertain
their rights in the situation, declared the publication
a nuisance, and ordered the mayor, who was Joseph
Smith, to abate it. The mayor, in turn, issued an
order to the city marshal "to destroy the printing
press from whence issued the *Nauvoo Expositor* and
pi the type of said printing establishment in the street,
and burn all the *Expositors* and libelous handbills
found in the establishment." This, the marshal did,
and so reported on his return on the same day.

Results followed quickly. Two days later Constable David Bettisworth called on the mayor and
served a writ on him and the members of the council.
They were jointly charged with having "committed a
riot at and within the county aforesaid" on the tenth
day of June. And they were ordered to appear before Justice Thomas Morrison, at Carthage, *"or some
other justice of the peace."* On June 13 a mass meeting of "the citizens of Hancock county" was held in
Carthage, at which, on the representation of Francis
M. Higbee, one of the owners of the *Nauvoo Expositor*,
resolutions were passed against *all Mormons* in the
county. One of these resolutions read: "As a community we feel anxious, when possible, to redress our
grievances by legal remedies; but the time has now
arrived when the law has ceased to be a protection
to our lives and property. A mob at Nauvoo, under
a city ordinance, has violated the highest privilege in
government; and to seek redress in the ordinary mode
would be utterly ineffectual."

Here is a clue to the assassination of Joseph and
Hyrum Smith. How could the lives and property of
citizens outside Nauvoo be in danger through an act
of the city council, performed in a strictly lawful way?
And why should a mass meeting be held in Carthage,

to resolve, by admittedly illegal means, that "the adherents of Smith should be driven from the surrounding settlements into Nauvoo," that "the prophet and his miscreant adherents should then be demanded at their (the Mormons') hands," and that "if not surrendered, a war of extermination should be waged to the entire destruction, if necessary for our protection, of his adherents?"

That the Prophet, with other leading Mormons, saw the situation in its true light, is evident from a letter to the governor, to this effect: "The citizens of this county who do not reside in Nauvoo, and those of other counties, have indeed no interest of a personal kind at stake in this matter. There are no persons disturbing them, nor going to do so; and this great excitement does savor of something else than a regard for the laws. Why not let the parties, as in all other cases of the kind, settle their difficulties as the laws of the country in such cases have provided?"

The mayor and his fellow councilmen were determined at this time not to go to Carthage. To have gone there would mean certain death at the hands of a mob. For those who had attended the mass meeting referred to were fully armed. The Prophet, in a letter to Governor Ford, wrote: "If your Excellency is not satisfied, and shall not be satisfied after reading the whole proceedings which will be forthcoming soon, and shall demand an investigation of our municipality before Judge Pope, or any legal tribunal at the Capitol, you have only to write your wishes, and we will be forthcoming. We will not trouble you to fill out a writ or send an officer for us." This letter is dated June 14. Two days later, on the advice of Judge Jesse B. Thomas, a non-Mormon, the mayor decided that he would be tried before Esquire Daniel H. Wells, also a non-Mormon justice of the peace. It would satisfy the writ on which he and the seventeen others had been arrested. The trial, which was held on June 17, would be before "some other justice of the peace." The trial was held and the defendant acquitted.

On several occasions Mayor Smith urged the governor to come to Nauvoo and make an official investigation. This Governor Ford finally decided to do. But, instead of going to Nauvoo, he went to Carthage, where there were hundreds of men known to be seeking the Prophet's life! June 21st brought Mayor Smith a letter from the governor, requesting that "you will send me at this place [Carthage] one or more well-informed and discreet persons, who will be capable of laying before me your version of the matter, and of receiving from me such explanations and resolutions as may be determined upon." In response to this request the mayor delegated Dr. John M. Bernhisel, Councilman John Taylor, and Dr. Willard Richards. On the following day Governor Ford wrote to the mayor: "I require any and all of you who are or shall be accused, to submit yourselves to be arrested by the same constable, by virtue of the same warrant and be tried before the same magistrate whose authority has heretofore been resisted. *Nothing short of this can vindicate the dignity of violated law and allay the just excitement of the people.*" And he added, "I will guarantee the safety of all such persons as may be brought to this place from Nauvoo either for trial or as witnesses for the accused."

To this Mayor Smith replied: "We dare not come, though your Excellency promises protection. Yet, at the same time, you have expressed fears that you could not control the mob, in which case we are left to the mercy of the merciless. Sir, we dare not come, for our lives would be in danger, and we are guilty of no crime."

Midnight of June 22 the Prophet crossed the

river to Iowa, with the intention of going to the
Rocky Mountains. His brother Hyrum, Dr. Richards,
and Orin Porter Rockwell were with him. Already,
after a prolonged investigation into the feasibility of
the project, he had decided to move his people there.
But on the following day, as he and his companions
were packing for the journey, he received a note from
his wife, urging him to stand for trial, and three
"friends" accused him of cowardice in deserting his
people in their hour of need. No one knew better
than President Smith that he, and only he, was the
target of the enemy rifle, But he said, "If my life
is of no value to my friends, it is of no value to myself!" And immediately he dictated a letter to Dr.
Richards, informing the governor that he was on his
way to Carthage.

There is no doubt that the Prophet had a strong
premonition of his death, and this premonition was
confirmed by threats on his life that came almost
daily from Carthage. To Hyrum, on the occasion of
his being accused of cowardice, he said, "We shall
be butchered!" And the last entry in his journal
reads: "I told Stephen Markham that if I and Hyrum
were ever taken again [he had been arrested and
acquitted thirty-seven times], we should be massacred,
or I was not a prophet of God." To some men, on
the way to Carthage, he remarked, "I am going like
a lamb to the slaughter." No one doubts to-day that
Joseph Smith could have saved his life by going west.

* * * * *

The mayor and thirteen others were taken before
Justice R. F. Smith at Carthage for trial on the charge
of riot, of which charge they had been freed by Squire
Wells. After some argument between the council for
the prosecution and that for the defence, the men were
bound over to the next term of the circuit court, in the
the sum of five hundred dollars each, a number of

well known persons in Nauvoo going their bond.
This should have been an end of the proceedings, but
on the twenty-fifth, Constable Bettisworth served a
writ on Joseph, in which he was accused of *treason!*
And he was ordered to appear for trial before the said
Smith, a justice of the peace! A similar writ was
served on Hyrum.

Later Constable Bettisworth appeared at the
lodgings of Joseph and Hyrum and requested them to
go to jail. Astonished at this demand, they insisted
on knowing his authority for this unwarranted pro-
cedure. Reluctantly he showed them a mittimus, in
which was this amazing phrase: "Whereas Joseph
and Hyrum Smith . . . have been arrested . . . for
the crime of treason, and *have been brought before me
for trial, which trial has been necessarily postponed
by reason of the absence of the material witnesses* . . .
(It was the trial on the charge of riot which had
been postponed.) Therefore, I command you, in the
name of the people, to receive said Joseph Smith and
Hyrum Smith into your custody in the jail, there to
remain until discharged by due course of law."

Governor Ford was appealed to, but he said that
he "did not think it within the sphere of his duty to
interfere, as they were in the hands of the civil law."
That is what he told the attorneys for the defence.
But to Justice Smith, who was also captain of a troop
in the militia, the governor said, "You have the Carthage Greys at your command." Smith, therefore, acting
in his capacity of justice, issued a false and illegal
mittimus, and then, in his capacity of captain of the
militia, proceeded to enforce this strange document.
The Smiths were thereupon taken to the county jail.

June 26th and 27th were spent by the prisoners
and their companions, John Taylor and Willard Richards, in an effort to induce the governor to inter-
vene in this muddle of legal red tape. Rumors were

rife that the Smiths were to be killed. "There is nothing against these men," said one rumor; "the law cannot touch them, but powder and ball will!" The governor knew of these threats, yet he took no measures whatever to protect the prisoners. On the contrary, he went to Nauvoo, away from the scene of impending murder. In doing this he broke two promises—to take the Prophet with him, if he went to the Mormon city, and to see that the prisoners were protected. He left them to their fate.

That fate overtook them at about five o'clock on the afternoon of the 27th. In the jail at the time were Joseph Smith, Hyrum Smith, John Taylor, and Dr. Willard Richards. "There was a little rustling at the outer door of the jail, and a cry of surrender, and also a discharge of three or four firearms followed instantly. The Doctor glanced an eye by the curtains of the window, and saw about a hundred armed men around the door. . . . The mob encircled the building, and some of them rushed by the guards up the flight of stairs, burst open the door, and began the work of death."

A ball struck Hyrum, and he fell on his back on the floor, exclaiming, "I am a dead man!" John Taylor was severely wounded. When Hyrum fell, Joseph exclaimed, "Oh, dear brother Hyrum!" and shortly afterwards sprang to the window. Two balls pierced him from the door, and one entered his right breast from without. Thereupon he fell out exclaiming, "O Lord, my God!" Dr. Richards escaped unhurt—miraculously, as he thought.

The dastardly deed was over in two minutes!

Next day the bodies of the dead were taken to Nauvoo. But only half a dozen people remained in Carthage; they had fled in the fear that the Mormons would rise against them as soon as it should be known that their leaders had been shot. But the Mormons were too sorrowful and had too much self control to kill their enemies; they awaited God's judgments.

Chapter XIII

AFTERMATH OF THE MARTYRDOM

On the death of Joseph Smith two problems faced the leaders of the Church. One was to keep the organization from falling to pieces, and the other was to conciliate the enemy so that there might not have to be another migration. In the first case they were successful, but in the second they failed.

As a matter of fact, the question of consolidating the organization presented little difficulty. It loomed large, however, for a time.

There are three leading quorums of priesthood in the Church. These are (1) the First Presidency of three, (2) the Twelve Apostles, and (3) the First Quorum of Seventy. With the death of the Prophet, of course, the First Presidency was dissolved, for, as he himself put it, "where I am not, there is no First Presidency." The tragedy in Carthage, therefore left the Twelve Apostles in full charge of the Church in all the world. This law of succession was not so clear then, however, as it is to-day. For the situation had come upon the Church very suddenly, and many members did not know the order of the Church. The situation had never appeared before in the history of the organization.

The president of the quorum of apostles at this time was Brigham Young. Until 1838 Thomas B. Marsh had been head of this group of officers, but Marsh, in those disturbed days in Missouri, had been carried away by the spirit of apostasy, and had been dropped, not only from this quorum, but also from the Church. Later he returned to the Church, but he never regained his position among the apostles. David

W. Patten, as we know, was second on the list of apostles, but Patten had been killed in the Battle of Crooked River, in Missouri. And this left in charge of the second quorum of the Church the man who was third on the list when the quorum was first organized.

Brigham Young was born in Vermont, June 1, 1801. He was, therefore, four and a half years older than the Prophet. His educational advantages were extremely meager. He had only eleven days of schooling in all. The last child in a family of nine children, he set out for himself on his career of carpenter, painter and glazier at sixteen years of age. Before joining Mormonism he was a Methodist. After his marriage to Miriam Works at the age of twenty-three he moved to New York, settling in Cayuga county and pursuing his vocation. Later, however, he moved to Mendon, Monroe county, in the same state. In the spring of 1830 he had read the *Book of Mormon*, which had been brought into the neighborhood by Samuel H. Smith, brother of the Prophet. Although greatly impressed by the new movement, he did not become a member of the Church till the spring of 1832, two years afterwards. It was not long till the entire Young family embraced the cause. Not until the autumn of the year of his baptism did Brigham Young meet the Prophet. This was in Kirtland, whither he and a bosom companion, Heber C. Kimball, had gone to see the head of the Church. From this time on the history of Brigham Young and the history of Mormonism were closely intertwined.

All the world knows the sterling qualities of this great man—his keen intelligence, which enabled him to make quick and proper adjustments both on his own behalf and on behalf of his people; his great executive and administrative ability, by which he became the greatest pioneer in Western America; his driving energy, which gave him power to succeed

The First Presidency and Twelve Apostles in 1853
These men had previously been intimately associated with Joseph Smith

Left to right:—First row: Heber C. Kimball, Brigham Young, Willard Richards.

Second row: Orson Hyde, Parley P. Pratt, Orson Pratt, Wilford Woodruff.

Third row: John Taylor, George A. Smith, Amasa M. Lyman, Ezra T. Benson.

Four row: Charles C. Rich, Lorenzo Snow, Erastus Snow, Franklin D. Richards.

where others might have failed. The Latter-day Saints knew him in his more intimate qualities—his attention to details; his trenchant, forthright English; his sympathy for poor people; his immense courage in a crisis; and his knowledge of spiritual truth, together with his understandable way of putting his religious views.

In most respects Brigham Young was markedly different from Joseph Smith. The Prophet's task was to lay the foundation; the great pioneer's, to build on that foundation. Joseph Smith established the lines of thought and growth along which Mormonism must develop if it would fulfil its destiny. Brigham Young found a home in the Great West for his people, and it was during his administration that the new movement was introduced to nations that theretofore had not known about it. The Prophet was a large man physically; he stood six feet without shoes and weighed two hundred twelve pounds. President Young was of medium height and, in his later years, tipped the scales at two hundred pounds. The founder of Mormonism was of a reflective, contemplative mind, in the main; his successor, of the active, administrative, practical type. The two men were, therefore, complements of each other, each fitted for a particular work.

*   *   *   *   *

When President Smith was murdered in Carthage jail, all the apostles, excepting John Taylor and Willard Richards, were away from home. So also were nearly all the other outstanding men of Nauvoo. Most of them were electioneering for Joseph Smith, who, as already stated, was a candidate for the presidency of the United States. On learning of the death of their leader, these men all hurried to Nauvoo by the nearest route. Meantime, the bodies of the martyred Prophet and Patriarch having been buried secretly, the faithful Saints found themselves for the moment shepherdless. But men soon appeared who would choose to lead them.

One of these was Sidney Rigdon. Rigdon, as we know, had been first counselor in the First Presidency of the Church. But he had gradually become indifferent, in consequence of which he had been rejected by the Prophet, and another, Amasa M. Lyman, had been chosen in his place. And then, too, Rigdon had moved to Pennsylvania to live. But now, on hearing of the death of his leader, he had hurried to Nauvoo. Capitalizing on the great love of the Saints for the Prophet, Rigdon said that no man could fill Joseph Smith's place. The Church must be built up to him, and he, Rigdon, would serve as "guardian" of the Church for that purpose!

Then there was James J. Strang, who first comes into notice here. An extremely able man and lawyer, Strang was ambitious for place and power. But he, unlike Rigdon, would be prophet, seer, and revelator of the Church, taking the place of Joseph Smith. Indeed, he asserted that the Prophet had set him apart to succeed in the leadership of the Church. Besides, he claimed to have had a vision on the subject.

And, finally, there was William Smith. William was a brother of the Prophet and one of the apostles, a member of the original quorum. His claim, however, did not come till some time later, after he had been made patriarch in the place of his brother Hyrum. The notice in the local paper announcing his elevation stated that William had been made patriarch "over" the Church, instead of "to" the Church. This probably gave him an idea that the office of patriarch and that of president were one and the same.

In those times news and people traveled very slowly. It was not till August 6, 1844, that a majority of the apostles reached Nauvoo. The quorum then comprised Brigham Young, Heber C. Kimball, Orson Hyde, Parley P. Pratt, William B. Smith, Orson Pratt, John E. Page, John Taylor, Wilford Woodruff, George A. Smith, Willard Richards, and Lyman Wight. Only Elders Page and William Smith had not arrived on the scene by August 6th. Two days later a meeting was held in the Grove at which the apostles were sustained as the presiding quorum of the Church, with Brigham Young as its president. President Young laid before the people the situation. "I will tell you," he said, "who your leaders or guardians will be—the Twelve, I at their head." And one of those who were at this gathering said later, "This was said with the voice of the Prophet. I thought it was he." Others have testified to the same thing— that it was the voice and the appearance of the Prophet.

Of course, that settled the question as to who would lead the Church—settled it, that is, in all but a few minds. The Twelve had been appointed by revelation as the second group of presiding officers in the Church, and now the people sustained them in this position. On that day it was decided that the Cause was greater than any man. And in sustaining the Twelve as the leaders of the Church, the people rejected, in this action, every other claimant to leadership—Rigdon, Strang, and Smith.

* * * * *

Not so much success was met with in the second problem that faced the apostles on the death of Joseph Smith—the conciliation of the non-Mormon population in Hancock county. For presently, after the sensation of the Prophet's death had calmed somewhat, an anti-Mormon party arose again, determined, it seems, to repeat the history of Missouri and expel the Saints from Illinois.

On the death of the Prophet there naturally followed a lull in the storm of opposition to the Mormon people. Everyone was stunned by the tragedy. A double murder had been committed, and it had been committed, too, by men under arms for the state. Moreover, the governor had more than once pledged his word, as the chief executive, that the prisoners would be protected. And so opposition to the Mormons subsided for a time, partly through fear and apprehension of consequences, partly through curiosity as to what would become of Mormonism, now that its founder had been taken.

There was no need for fear and apprehension, however, for the element that brought about the death of the brothers Smith saw to it that nothing was done to punish their murderers. A trial was held in Carthage in May, 1845, of those who had been indicted in the preceding October, but it was a farce. There was little doubt as to the identity of the murderers, but public sentiment was so strong against the Mormons that the judge instructed the jury to bring in a verdict of "not guilty." Besides, armed men, according to John Hay, threatened witnesses, attorneys, and even the judge.

But the Saints had no doubt as to themselves or their cause. The work was of God, and in the end would triumph. Nothing could stop its progress. So the apostles carried on with as much energy and enthusiasm as before. With abounding vitality they builded on the foundation laid by the Prophet.

They hastened to complete the temple. In January, 1841, as we have seen, the Prophet had received a revelation in which the Saints were commanded to erect a House of the Lord on pain of being "rejected with their dead." In April, of that year, the corner stone had been laid; in November of the same year the font had been dedicated, and baptisms for the dead, which had been performed in the river, were discontinued there and performed in the font.   But, in October, 1845, the general conference of the Church was held in the assembly room of the building, so far had it progressed, and in December, 1845, "endowments" were received there by hundreds of Saints—that is, temple ordinances for the living and baptisms for the dead.

In order, however, that the temple might be built, funds had to be obtained.   Hence, in letters which the apostles sent out to the Church generally everyone was advised to "proceed immediately to tithe himself" and pay the money "into the hands of the Twelve or of such bishops as have been appointed by them."   And, in addition, the Saints were counseled to cultivate their farms and to manufacture such articles as might be turned into cash.

Spiritual matters, too, received attention.   Steps were taken by the apostles to speed missionary work and to steady the organization in the United States, Canada, and England.   The duty of carrying the message of the gospel to the world was placed definitely on the shoulders of the Seventy. "If the people will let us alone," said President Young at this time, "we will convert the world, and if they persecute us, we will do it quicker."   Also they "cut off the dead branches," not only at home, but abroad as well. And everywhere the missionaries sought to inform the members of the Church that the "keys of the kingdom" were still with the Church.   The test of fellowship, as stated by the head of the apostles, was belief in the prophetic calling of Joseph Smith. "Every spirit that confesses that Joseph Smith is a prophet, that he lived and died a prophet, and that the *Book of Mormon* is true, is of God, and every spirit that does not, is of anti-Christ."   It was a thoroughly Christian spirit in which every one worked—helping the poor, strengthening the weak, and fostering love and service.

Notwithstanding the fact that the Mormon people minded their own business, the anti-Mormon organization, after it became evident that the murderers of the Prophet would not be punished and that Mormonism would not come to an end with the death of its founder, began again its activity, with the avowed purpose of driving the Saints from the state. We shall see how well it succeeded.

Chapter XIV

THE MORMONS AGAIN WITHOUT A HOME

Long before water began to run and grass to grow the Saints were on their way to the Great West, to build another home for themselves. On February 4, 1846, the first covered wagons crossed from the Illinois to the Iowa side of the Mississippi river.

It seems that the average man in that great trek did not know the destination of these twenty thousand and more Latter-day Saints. He knew that there was a "peaceful, sleepy population" on the Pacific coast, in California, where Spanish priests were endeavoring to instil into the minds of the Mexicans and the American Indians there the Christian standards of thought and work, and that there were the beginnings of settlements in the silent territory of "the continuous woods, where rolled the Oregon," of which the poet Bryant spoke a little earlier than this.

He knew that west of the Mississippi lay the great prairie land, that west of the prairie land towered the Rocky Mountains, and that beyond these were some deserts, some forests, and then the sea. He knew, too, that from Independence, Missouri, the Oregon Trail, made originally by the foot of the red man and deepened by the foot of the buffalo, threaded the flowered plains of Iowa, the shifting sands of the desert, and the timbered gorges of the mountains, past the famous landmarks of Chimney Rock, Fort Laramie, Independence Rock, Sweetwater, Devil's Gate, and Fort Bridger, and over the hills to the ocean—a truly wonderful trail, the longest in history. And he knew, finally, that in all this

vast silent country the echoes were awakened only
by the voice of the trapper in quest of fur, the war
cry of the skulking red man, the yelp of the wolf and
the coyote, and the bellow of the innumerable bison
of the plains.

But the leaders knew where they were going.
Their destination had been chosen for them by the
Prophet Joseph Smith before his death. We have seen
that the Prophet, just prior to his surrender to Governor Ford, was on the point of leaving for the West,
when accused of cowardice in leaving his people.
We have seen also that he thereupon went direct
to Carthage, where he and his brother Hyrum were
murdered by a mob. Before that, however, he had
appointed a committee to select a place in the midst
of the Rockies, of which he had prophesied, and to
point out the general route to be taken. And it was
this information, obtained from books and maps,
that these leaders used in reaching the place where
they were to bring their people and establish them in
settlements. The positiveness with which President
Young chose the way is the best evidence we have or
need that he knew where that place was.

* * * * *

"The people of Iowa," wrote Colonel Thomas L.
Kane, "have told me that from morning to night they
[the Mormons] passed westward like an endless pro-
cession. They did not seem greatly out of heart,
they said; but at the top of every hill, before they
disappeared, were to be seen looking back, like banished Moors, on the abandoned homes and the far-
seen temple and its glittering spire." From February
4th till almost the end of the year of 1846 long trains
of covered wagons might have been seen jerking their
heavy way across the prairie.

The first wagons, however, stayed for a few days
on what then went by the name of Sugar Creek,

about nine miles west of Nauvoo. Here there was a grove, where they camped. It had snowed just before this, and the ground was covered with a white blanket. Brushing away this covering, they pitched their tents. That night, with a falling thermometer, nine babies were born. The first stage of the journey took them to the banks of the Missouri river.

Entrance to Kanesville or Council Bluffs

The earlier days of the trek were distressing in the extreme. Snow lay on the earth to a depth of six or eight inches. At the camping grounds, after the men and animals had been there for a time, the place, as one of the travelers tells us in his journal, became a veritable "slush of snow and mud, and nowhere to sit or lie but in water and snow." The first night out, this man says, his wife received an invitation "to lie on some corn stalks"—an invitation which she eagerly accepted. The husband, with another man, lay "on a single blanket on the snow," which, when they awoke in the night, had "frozen to their sides," the weather having turned bitterly cold, so that they were compelled to sit up before the fire till dawn. At another camping place, later on, it rained for a whole week.

Presently "the snow had all gone, and the ground was nearly covered with water." Then it was that the wagons, many of them, broke down or got stuck in the mud, necessitating the doubling up of teams. For there were no roads, the way the Saints took, between the two rivers. They did not follow the Oregon Trail because some of their old-time enemies from Missouri were taking that trail. At one time it took three yoke of oxen to pull five hundred pounds. Often women and children, as well as men, had to walk through the mud and slush. Occasionally fierce winds tore to shreds the canvas of their tents and wagons. The time of the spring rains and freshets over, though, the journey was not so unpleasant.

Obtaining food for man and beast these first days was a problem. In order to undertake this trek it was required that each family of five should have one wagon, three yoke of oxen or teams, two cows, two beef cattle, three sheep, one thousand pounds of flour, twenty-four pounds of sugar, a tent and bedding, seeds, farm tools, and a rifle—about two hundred dollars' worth in all. But many did not have this, especially the food. Indeed, one time eight hundred men, heads of families, reported that they did not even have two weeks' provisions on hand.

For three weeks this group lived on boiled corn alone. When, on one occasion, some one gave them a little flour and bacon, they considered it "quite a treat." Once, having a rifle which he knew how to use, one of the men ventured out on a hunt, and brought home five fox squirrels and two pheasants, which, when cooked, the captain enjoyed with him and the family. Another time he received some venison in return for the use of his gun, which a man borrowed and with which a deer was killed. If the company stayed at a given place for any considerable length of time, men would be sent over the line into Missouri to look for work. One time the man we are speaking about "husked corn on shares to feed ourselves and horses." On other occasions he helped to "build a house," receiving "some corn and beans and pork" for his labor, and cleared a field for some grain. Until the grass began to grow the only food for the animals was a very little corn and the buds and branches and bark of trees.

The organization of the "Camp of Israel" was simple. At the head stood Brigham Young. This was before he was made president of the Church. Under him were two general divisions of the camp. Of one he took charge; Heber C. Kimball managed the other. Then there were groups of a hundred, of fifty, and of ten, each with a captain. (The words "hundred," "fifty," and "ten" were applied to wagons, not to persons.) And this is the way the emigrants traveled till they reached their temporary quarters on the plains.

It was the spirit, however, that distinguished this movement of a people. The keynote was sounded by President Young before they had gone very far. "If any man," he said "shall seek to build up himself he shall have no power, and his folly shall be made manifest." This sentence is from a revelation which he received on the way west. (*Doctrine and Covenants,* section 136.) And he admonished the Saints to fulfil their "pledges to one another," to "keep themselves from evil," and to refrain from contention, evil-speaking, and drunkenness. Their words, he added, should tend "to edify one another;" they should return what they borrowed, and what they found that had been lost; and they should be diligent in preserving what they had, so as to be "wise stewards" to the Lord. In joy they might sing and dance, "with prayer and thanksgiving;" in sorrow they were to "call upon the Lord with supplication." And they were to fear no enemies.

Moreover, the spirit of teamwork characterized the movement. At every favorable spot in Iowa houses were built, ground was plowed and planted, and then left for those who followed to enjoy. At Garden Grove, for instance, in response to a call, three hundred fifty-nine men presented themselves for work. Of these, one hundred were appointed to cut down and trim trees, ten to build fences, twelve to dig wells, ten to build bridges, and the rest to clear the land, to plow the ground, and to plant seed. This having been done, the company moved on, without a thought for themselves. To be sure, men were left in charge of the buildings and the crops, with a presiding officer. But it was with the distinct understanding that those who occupied the houses and harvested the crops were to turn into the general storehouse what was left after the amount necessary to live had been deducted.

Also the spirit of religion prevailed in all the divisions of the camp. The day opened and closed with prayer and other devotional exercises. Usually this was a matter for each family to attend to, but sometimes it became a group affair. That a man did not pray in his family was generally regarded as sufficient cause for distrust.

* * * * *

Mention has already been made of the settlement of the Mormons at a place which they called Garden Grove. It was not intended, of course, that this settlement should be permanent. It was too far from the Missouri river. But it would serve for a

time as a natural base of supplies for the oncoming
train of emigrants. And that was what it came to be.

Slightly different was it with the next westward settlement made by the Saints—Mount Pisgah.
Situated on an elevation, it was made one of the
main towns established by the Mormons on their
way west. Thousands lived here and the settlement
had presiding officers. The first of these officers
were William Huntington, president, and Ezra T.
Benson and Charles C. Rich, counselors. Not long
after this President Huntington passed away in the
epidemic of chills and fever that swept over the place,
and Elder Benson was presently elevated to the apostleship; whereupon Elder Rich was made president.
This settlement continued, with a somewhat shifting
population, till the early fifties, when all its inhabitants left for the new home in the mountains.

More substantial was Winter Quarters, on the
west side of the Missouri. Here was located the main
body of Mormons. The houses were mostly of logs,
though some of them were "dugouts"—excavations
made into a hill side and roofed over. In this place
the Saints lived, for the most part, during the winter
of 1846-7 and that also of 1847-8. Here, too, there
was a log tabernacle, used mainly for religious gather-
ings, and there were stores also, kept and owned by
individuals. The stock of merchandise, of course,
came from the settlements east of the Mississippi
river, and was hauled over the prairies by ox teams.

In all the Mormon settlements on the plains between the two rivers there was much sickness and
many deaths. At Mount Pisgah, for instance, chills
and fever visited the town. Literally hundreds came
down with the disease. Between five and six hundred died. Then there was scurvy, a disease marked
by livid spots under the skin, with swollen and bleed-
ing gums and great prostration, caused by the con-

tinued use of salt meats without fresh vegetables. There were many deaths, too, in Winter Quarters. It was from this point that the companies of trekkers left for Elkhorn, where they formed and organized for their journey to the mountains.

Such, then, was the picture of the Mormons crossing the prairie between the Mississippi and the Missouri, on their famous trek to the Rocky Mountains. It might be likened to a cord between two and three hundred miles long, with knots in it, the knots standing for settlements. This cord would stretch out between the two rivers during most of the year 1846. There would be, in September of this year, a group of about one thousand Saints, mainly the sick and the aged, on the west bank of the Mississippi. That would be one knot. The others would be Garden Grove and Mount Pisgah, with Winter Quarters on the other end. Gradually the east end of this cord would be drawn up, till the most easterly end would be at Mount Pisgah.

That settlement on the west bank of the Mississippi should have a little attention here. These thousand helpless people are often called the "remnants." They were old men, women, and children who had been unable, on account of poverty, to make the journey to the Missouri in the regular companies, and they were left in Nauvoo pending the return of teams and wagons to convey them thither. It was thought they would be unmolested by the mob. But the Mormon leaders had over-estimated the humanity of their enemies in Hancock county.

Major Warren, who was decidedly unfriendly to the Mormons, visited Nauvoo. After this visit he issued a report and proclamation, in which he said that the Saints were moving with "all possible dispatch." And he added a warning for all those who wished the removal of the Mormons, whom he gra-

ciously called "good citizens," to "stay at home."
Yet these "good citizens" attacked Nauvoo in September, with the result that these poor people were
driven across the river. The enemy forces were under the direction of a man named Brockman, a preacher. The Mormons, under the command of Major
Clifford, who had been appointed by Governor Ford,
made what resistence they could, but to no effect.
The wagons of the Mormons were ransacked and
their contents scattered. Sick persons were not immune from harsh treatment. Moreover, the mob desecrated the temple, and plundered the homes not only
of the Saints but also of those who had purchased
homes from the Saints. Penniless, hungry, destitute,
these poor remnants presented a pitiful sight on the
west bank of the river. And their only food for
days consisted of quail, which they caught with
their hands.

Chapter XV

THE SAINTS FIND A NEW HOME

In June, 1846, there rode into the settlement of Mount Pisgah an officer of the United States army. His name was James Allen, and he held the rank of captain in the regular force. He had come to the Mormon settlements to raise a contingent of soldiers for the war that was going on with Mexico. He had been sent here by Colonel S. W. Kearney, of the United States Army.

Finding that many of the people had left Mount Pisgah, he sat down and wrote a letter to the Mormons on the trail. He wished, he said, to raise four or five companies of men, to serve for twelve months, with the regular pay of soldiers. In doing this he felt that "thus is offered to the Mormon people now —this year—an opportunity of sending a portion of their young and intelligent men to the ultimate destination of their whole people, and entirely at the expense of the United States, and this advance party can thus pave the way and look out the land for their brethren to come after them."

The situation at this time in all the camps of the Mormon people was anything but good. All of them, as a matter of fact, were poor as to earthly property. Most of their lands and houses they had been unable to sell at all, and much of what they had sold had been at a ridiculously low figure. The poorest of them had to be helped by those who were better off. In addition, many of the able bodied young men had gone to the non-Mormon settlements in adjoining states, to work and earn enough money to continue the journey west. Finally, it was the in-

tention of the leaders to take a hand-picked company
of men, to explore and prepare the way to the new
home in the mountains. The Saints could not, therefore, have been caught in a worse plight for raising
a battalion for the army.

As a matter of fact, however, the Mormon leaders
had solicited aid of the Federal government on
their westward trek. In January, 1846, Elder Jesse
C. Little had been sent to preside over the Eastern
States mission. He had been specially requested to
see whether he could not enlist the sympathies of
the President in Washington—James K. Polk—in the
forced migration of the Mormons. A letter which
he wrote to President Polk suggested that some "assistance" be given the people by the government and
hinted that their destination was "California," a
general name for the territory west of the Rocky
Mountains. The President's answer was to make this
call for volunteers. The leaders, of course, were
greatly surprised at this form of aid. Nevertheless
they accepted the idea.

President Young, when Captain Allen went to
see him, said that the government should have five
hundred men. And more than five hundred men
between the ages of eighteen and forty-five volunteered.

*   *   *   *   *

After a farewell party, with speeches and dancing
on some ground cleared for the purpose, the Mormon
Battalion set out for Fort Leavenworth. Here they
received about twenty one thousand dollars, one year
advanced pay for clothing. Part of this money they
sent to their families. They also contributed freely
to aid Elders Orson Hyde, Parley P. Pratt and John
Taylor, who were bound for England on missions.
The army officials who gave them the money were
greatly surprised that every one of the Battalion could

sign his own name. One out of every three of the
volunteers from Missouri had signed with a cross.

The first captain of the Mormon soldiers was
James Allen, who had drafted them. But presently
he died, much to the regret of the Battalion, and his
place was taken by Lieutenant A. J. Smith of the
regular army. Lieutenant Smith was arrogant, inefficient, and petty. The men did not like him. The
physician accompanying the troops had the same
characteristics. Their march took them in a south-
westerly direction to the old Spanish town of Santa
Fe, thence to the present city of El Paso, and across
the Gila and Colorado rivers to San Diego, California.

On leaving the Arkansas river, the commander
of the Battalion ordered that a number of families
of the volunteers, who had accompanied them thus far,
should go to Pueblo, a Mexican town, so as not to
delay the march to the west coast. And this was
done. We shall hear of these later on. At Santa Fe,
where Colonel Doniphan, an old friend of the Mormons, was in command, the arrival of the Battalion
was greeted with a salute of one hundred guns. Here
Colonel Phillip St. George Cook took charge. It
was he that conducted the Battalion the rest of the
way to the sea. They went through what the Colonel
termed a wilderness, without so much as a trail.
And he adds: "It [the Battalion] was enlisted too
much by families; some were too old—some feeble,
and some too young; it was embarrassed by many
women; it was undisciplined; it was much worn by
traveling on foot, and marching from Nauvoo." Nevertheless, Colonel Cook said after the journey had been
completed: "History may be searched in vain for an
equal march of infantry." The distance was approximately two thousand miles.

By the time the Battalion reached the coast the
war was over. They did not have to do any fighting.

This was, in fact, a promise made to them before they left Council Bluffs by President Young. Most of their work on the coast consisted, therefore, of digging wells, making brick, painting fences, and building houses—peace-time labor. They were mustered out of service in July, 1847.

For the present we shall take our leave of these men, to meet them again a little later.

*   *   *   *   *

Meantime, the work of preparing for another move westward went on at Winter Quarters. The call of the Battalion had hindered the preparations somewhat, and so it was necessary to change the plans that had been made. The trek was put back one year. It was now decided to select a few men only, to outfit these in the best way possible under the circumstances, and then to lead the way to the place in the Rocky Mountains which had been pointed out by the Prophet Joseph Smith. And this was done.

The pioneer company, as it is generally termed, comprised one hundred forty-eight persons in all— one hundred forty-three men, three women, and two children. This was the number that left Elkhorn. But it was not, as we shall see, the number that reached the valley of the Great Salt Lake. The company carried seeds of various kinds and farming utensils, so that land in the new home might be tilled as soon as the place was reached. Fortunately, just as the pioneer company was about to start west, Elder John Taylor arrived, bringing with him the sum of two thousand dollars in gold, which the Saints in Great Britain had contributed, and some scientific instruments for surveying purposes. Later these were used by Elder Orson Pratt, a practical surveyor, in laying out Salt Lake City. The company was divided into groups of officers in charge

"The Tragedy of Winter Quarters"
Monument at Winter Quarters, Nebraska, in Mormon Pioneer Cemetery
—Avard Fairbanks, Sculptor.

of each. It was necessary that order prevail in the undertaking.

The route followed by the pioneer company was along the Platte river to Fort Laramie. Here they crossed the stream and continued over the Oregon Trail to Fort Bridger. Leaving the Trail, they struck off to Echo Canyon, over Big and Little Mountain, into what is now called Emigration Canyon, and into the valley of Salt Lake. They were on the way from April 5th to July 24th, 1847. The distance covered by the company was about eleven hundred miles. An odometer, conceived and made by Orson Pratt and William Clayton, measured the distance from camp to camp.

This is the William Clayton whose memory is preserved in the song, "Come, Come, Ye Saints," which helped to keep up the spirit of the pioneers, not only in this first group, but in all other companies that crossed the plains with oxen and horses, and which the Saints still sing with great ferver. Elder Clayton was an English convert, one of the first. When he immigrated to America, he went directly to Nauvoo, where he became secretary to the Prophet. This song was composed—that is, the words of this song—before the Saints began the second stage of their journey to the mountains. Better than any other words, it expresses the situation in which the Mormon people found themselves on this memorable trek—their courage under stress, their fortitude in trying circumstances, their faith, their trust in God, and their hope for rest after the journey and in the hereafter. Following is the song in its entirety:

> Come, come, ye Saints, no toil nor labor fear,
>   But with joy wend your way;
> Tho' hard to you this journey may appear,
>   Grace shall be as your day.
> 'Tis better far for us to strive,
>   Our useless cares from us to drive;

Do this, and joy your hearts will swell—
    All is well! all is well!

Why should we mourn, or think our lot is hard?
    'Tis not so; all is right!
Why should we think to earn a great reward,
    If we now shun the fight?
Gird up your loins, fresh courage take,
    Our God will never us forsake;
And soon we'll have this tale to tell—
    All is well! all is well!

We'll find the place which God for us prepared,
    Far away, in the West;
Where none shall come to hurt or make afraid;
    There the Saints will be blessed.
We'll make the air with music ring,
    Shout praises to our God and King;
Above the rest these words we'll tell—
    All is well! all is well!

And should we die before our journey's through,
    Happy day! all is well!
We then are free from toil and sorrow, too;
    With the just we shall dwell!
But if our lives are spared again
    To see the Saints their rest obtain,
O how we'll make this chorus swell—
    All is well! all is well!

A little beyond Fort Laramie, now in Wyoming,
the pioneer company was joined by seventeen other
persons. These were the Saints who had come originally from Mississippi and who had wintered with
some members of the Battalion at Pueblo. In five
wagons they had traveled from that Spanish town
to Fort Laramie, in an effort to overtake the pioneers.
There were other Mississippi Saints, but they had remained in Pueblo. On the arrival of the seventeen
at the pioneer camp, four of the pioneers were sent
to Pueblo to guide the rest to the western home.
Later—on July 1—the company was joined by thirteen of the Battalion, who had come west to go to the
mountains. In this small group of Mississippi Saints
were six women, and these entered the Salt Lake

valley with the pioneer company. The main entrance into the valley was effected on July 24, 1847. Three days before this, however, Orson Pratt and Erastus Snow had descended into the valley.

One of the singular things about this pioneer company is the spirit which characterized its leader and which he sought to give to the members of it.

Both Wilford Woodruff and Erastus Snow declare that President Young had had a vision of the valley prior to his seeing it with the physical eye. They received this information from the President himself. It was for this reason that he exclaimed, when he first set eyes on the valley of the Salt Lake from the eastern hill, "This is the place!" This is why, too, he regarded the undertaking as sacred.

On the way west some members of the company engaged in card-playing and other objectionable activities, in order to pass away the time in camp. When this sort of thing had gone beyond his patience, President Young called the men together and talked to them. Elder Woodruff represents the President as saying this:

"I had rather risk myself among the savages with ten men who are men of faith, men of mighty prayer, men of God, than to be with a whole camp when they forget the Lord and turn their hearts to folly and wickedness. Yes, I would rather be alone, and I am resolved not to go any farther with the camp unless you will consent to humble yourselves before the Lord and serve him. . . . How would you look if they should know your conduct and ask you what you did when you went out to seek Zion and find a resting place for the Saints where the Kingdom of God could be reared and her banners unfurled for the nations to gather to?"

After that there was more decorum in the camp.

Chapter XVI

THE NEW HOME OF THE MORMONS

The scene which greeted the members of the pioneer company from the eastern rim of the mountain was anything but attractive, unless looked at with the eyes of the imagination.

One of the women, on reaching the valley and looking it over, remarked that weary as she was, yet she would gladly go another thousand miles rather than stay there. This sentiment was echoed by another of the women. Nor can this be wondered at. For there was hardly a tree or other green thing to be seen anywhere. Surrounded by mountains and a lake of salt, the valley was largely a desert, where, it would seem, nothing could be made to grow.

The men reacted differently to the scene. That was because they viewed it with the eyes of the mind and spirit. To Brigham Young it was, of course, "the place." Others of the apostles thought the same. Said Wilford Woodruff: "I was joyfully disappointed." He had expected less than he beheld. And he went into raptures over what he saw. He was thinking of the predictions made concerning this new home by the Prophet some years before and of the words of Brigham Young, as the two beheld the valley for the first time from the eastern mountain.

* * * * *

It was Saturday when the last of the pioneer company descended into the basin. The next day, therefore, the group, now numbering one hundred seventy-four persons in all, held religious services.

Already the land had been dedicated by the apostle Orson Pratt. This had been one of the first things done by the advance guard of the pioneers. Also some land had been plowed and planted to potatoes and other products. It was hoped that there would be a crop before the frosts overtook the colony. In order, however, to plow the ground the men turned the water from the creek over the soil, to soften it enough to receive the plow.

Two services were held on this Sunday, the first in the Salt Lake valley. At the afternoon meeting President Young, who was ill, made a short address. "He told the brethren," we are informed, "that they must not work on Sunday; that they would lose five times as much as they would gain by it. None was to hunt on that day; and there should not any man dwell among us who would not observe these rules. They might go and dwell where they pleased, but they should not dwell with us. He said also that no man who came here should buy any land; that he had none to sell, but that every man should have his land measured out to him for city and farming purposes. He might till it as he pleased, but he must be industrious and take care of it." There should be no private ownership of the timber or of the streams that came down from the mountains.

*   *   *   *   *

Sunday being over, no time was lost by the pioneers in exploring the new home and in establishing themselves there.

On Monday a dozen men went out from the camp on what has since been called City Creek into various parts of the valley. President Young and others visited some hot springs at the north end of the basin. This same group also ascended a mount, to the northeast of the camp. On President Young's remarking that it would be a good place to lift up an ensign for the nations, in fulfillment of Isaiah's prophecy, they thereupon named the mount "Ensign Peak," a name

"As Brigham Young Saw It"

Entrance Into the Salt Lake Valley of the Pioneer Company

—Painting by J. B. Fairbanks

which it still bears. Other groups went to other parts of the valley and, on their return, made reports of what they had discovered.

Meantime it was decided to lay out a townsite. This was on the 28th. The settlement should be called Great Salt Lake City. The word "great," of course, applied to the lake, but in later years it was dropped from the name. The surveying was done under the direction of Orson Pratt. It had been decided to follow the plan of the proposed "City of Zion," platted by Joseph Smith in Independence, Missouri— a city that was never built. Each block was divided into lots of about a quarter-acre, except the central block which was set aside for public buildings. The farms were to be on the outside. "Let every man," President Young urged, "cultivate his own lot and set out every kind of fruit and shade tree and beautify the city." The streets were wide and crossed one another as right angles.

On this same day President Young and the apostles walked a short distance from their camp to a piece of ground between the forks of City Creek. This site was set apart for the building of a temple.

Before the week was ended there were more arrivals in the valley. These were some members of the Mormon Battalion, under the command of Captain James Brown, numbering about two hundred. They had wintered at Pueblo. At once they began the erection of a willow bowery—the first place of public worship in Utah. Later the first theatrical plays were presented in this structure. It consisted of a quadrangle of poles set in the ground and bound together at the top by other poles, roofed over with still more poles and branches of trees. It protected those who met there from the sun.

All told, the number of people now in Salt Lake valley was about four hundred. But in August,

1847, nearly half of this number returned to Winter Quarters to bring their families. Among these was President Young, with all the apostles who had come west. Beginning in October, however, about eighteen hundred others entered the basin. This large company was led by apostles Parley P. Pratt and John Taylor. One of the groups in it, which was under the direction of Charles C. Rich, brought some military equipment from the East.

Meantime a fort had been built for the protection of the Saints from the Indians. This was a large square, the walls of which,. for the most part, consisted of the backs of the log houses. These walls were made of logs and sun-dried bricks, and were nine feet high and twenty-seven inches thick. The roofs of the houses consisted of poles covered with brush and earth. After the arrival of the first company two more squares were added. And here the two thousand pioneers spent their first winter in the valley.

Before a part of the vanguard pioneer company took up their return journey to the Missouri river a conference of the Church was held. At this gathering there were only about four hundred persons, for the first large company was then on its way west. Here it was decided that a presidency and a high council be appointed, to preside over the Saints in the valley. The presidency comprised three men who were then on their way—John Smith, uncle of the Prophet Joseph Smith, Charles C. Rich, and John Young. Here, too, the river running through the valley was called the Jordan; it connects a fresh water lake with a salt water lake in a manner comparable with the Jordan in Palestine. Likewise, the valley itself here received a name. "This is a paradise to me, and one of the loveliest places I ever beheld," said Heber C. Kimball at this meeting. "I hope none of us will be left alive to pollute this land. I would rather die than act as inconsistently as many have in times past."

*   *   *   *   *

It was a precarious situation in which these pioneers found themselves during that first winter. They were a thousand miles from the nearest settlement to the east, and about eight hundred miles from the nearest settlement to the west. That they had not brought provisions enough to last them till the first harvest is evident from the fact that, before their crops matured, they had to resort to sego roots and thistle tops for food. There was great danger, too, that winter might prove too much for them, as that season of the year, with its deep snows and heavy frosts, was known to be severe. Besides, the whole colony stood in danger of being utterly destroyed by Indians. For, although the natives in the valley were mild enough, there were other tribes not far away who were rather ferocious.

Fortunately, more than one thing favored the little colony that first year. The winter was so mild that plowing, planting, and building were carried on during most of the time. And then, in addition, only the nearby natives visited them. There was little or no trouble from the Indians, therefore. But, most of all, the colony was fortunate in its leadership that first year. The presiding officers had had much experience in executive and administrative work among the Saints. Particularly was this true of Charles C. Rich. He had been brigadier-general in the Nauvoo Legion under the direction of Joseph Smith, who was its lieutenant-general, and he had presided over the Saints at Mount Pisgah on the plains.

In spite of its mildness that first winter called for some constructive work. Conciliatory measures were adopted with the natives. The trappers and fur-

traders were sought out and their good will cultivated. A group of men, under Captain Jefferson
Hunt, an officer in the Mormon Battalion, was dis-
patched to the valley of San Bernardino, to purchase
livestock for the Salt Lake settlers. Five thousand
acres of ground were plowed, and a good part of it
fenced. And a government, half political and half
religious, was set up with some specific rues of conduct and penalties.

The politico-religious government, adopted under
pressure of circumstances, deserves some attention
in particular, as expressing the character of the
Mormons for order and system.

A committee had been appointed, of which General Rich was chairman, to formulate some rules and
regulations. In December this committee reported.
The rules suggested by it, the committee explained,
were offered "in the absence of any organized juris-
diction of any territory, for the peace, welfare, and
good order of the community." One rule was that
every able-bodied man must work. If any man would
not do so, he was to be hailed before the judge and
pronounced a vagrant, and in that event he would
be forced to work and his earnings given to his dependents. Other rules regulated conduct. There were
rules about theft and robbery, drunkenness, and in-
fractions of the moral law. In some cases the lash
was to be applied—"not exceeding thirty-nine." They
were to be on the bare back. Also fines were imposed.
There is no record, however, of the whip having been
used.

Thus the first winter was passed by this Mormon
colony in the mountains. House-building, planting,
fencing, hauling timber, conciliating the Indians,
searching for new sources of food—these were the
principal occupations of the men folk in the Salt Lake
valley.

Chapter XVII

BUILDING A COMMONWEALTH

In the spring most of the families moved out of the fort. That had never been comfortable. It furnished but cramped quarters at best. A whole family had to live in one room, and when it rained the roof leaked. And so, as soon as they could safely do so, they went out on the land, where they could have room and fewer discomforts.

But spring and summer, also, had their drawbacks. When the corn, the peas, the beans, and the cucumbers pushed up their green stalks through the ground, a frost came and turned them black. And later on, when the wheat began to ripen in the big field, which had been plowed and fenced and tilled by common effort, crickets swarmed down from the canyons and devoured much of the grain. These pests would have destroyed the entire crop had it not been for the sea gulls. The birds ate their fill of the insects, then flew to nearby streams, where they spued them out, and, after they had repeated this work of salvation for a few days, the crickets all disappeared. This was a direct answer to the prayers of the colonists, for they had given up in despair after their own efforts had utterly failed. They had tried water, mops and other household utensils, and even fire—all to no purpose. Prayer had proved a surer weapon. In Utah, therefore, the gull is a sacred bird, protected by law, and on Temple Square, in Salt Lake City, is a stately column to commemorate the saving of those first crops to the settlers. This is perhaps the only monument in the world erected to a bird.

In the autumn of 1848 President Young returned

to the valley, with nearly twenty-five hundred people and thousands of animals. This brought the population to between four and five thousand inhabitants.

On this second trip west Brigham Young came as President of the Church, the position which the Prophet Joseph Smith had occupied. It was at Winter Quarters that he was chosen to this high place. He was selected by the apostles and sustained by the members of the Church generally at a meeting in the log tabernacle. He chose Heber C. Kimball for his first counselor and Willard Richards for his second. These now constituted the First Presidency of the Church, after an administration by the apostles of three and a half years. This action took three of the Twelve out of the quorum, and the apostasy of Lyman Wight increased the number of vacancies to four. These four places were presently filled by the ordination of four others to the apostleship as members of the quorum—Charles C. Rich, who at the time was president of the Salt Lake stake; Erastus Snow, Lorenzo Snow, and Franklin D. Richards. With the arrival of the First Presidency in the colony things moved swiftly and definitely forward.

* * * * *

First, room was made for those members of the Church who expected to gather with their people in the Rocky Mountains. For it was the intention to make extensive settlements in the West. At Nauvoo, for instance, there had been between twenty and twenty-five thousand Latter-day Saints, if we include the small settlements on the outskirts of the town. In Great Britain, according to a statement by Jesse C. Little to President Polk, there were forty thousand converts to the faith, and it was designed to bring these to the mountain home. And there must have been other thousands scattered throughout the United States and Canada. All these the Church leaders expected to distribute over an extensive triangle, whose sides comprised the Pacific Ocean, a line drawn from Salt Lake City to Los Angeles, and another line between Salt Lake City and San Francisco. Moreover, plans were in the making to bring emigrants from Europe by sea and over the Isthmus of Panama to San Diego. This is the "empire" so often spoken of as in the mind of the Mormon leaders.

In pursuance of this plan of colonization Amasa M. Lyman and Charles C. Rich went to California, partly to gather tithing from the Saints in that territory and partly to look about for good locations for settlements. For, besides some two hundred fifty members of the Mormon Battalion, there were two hundred thirty-five Saints, who had gone there by sea from New York City, in 1846, under the direction of Samuel Brannan. Elder Rich took the southern route to California; that is, he went by way of Los Angeles and the coast to San Francisco and Sacramento. The Saints in California were prospering by this time, for this was in the autumn of 1849, after the discovery of gold. The apostle was accompanied on his journey by twenty missionaries who were bound for the Sandwich Islands, now called the Hawaiian Islands. These men went part way with what has come to be known as the Death Valley Expedition of gold seekers, nearly all of whom perished in Death Valley or on the way there. The missionaries were saved from a horrible death, by their leaving the others and taking a different route.

By the time the second company of Mormons arrived in the Salt Lake Basin, in the fall of 1848, settlements had been made in what is now Davis County, Utah. In 1848 Captain James Brown bought the Goodyear Grant, in the Weber valley, for the Battalion men, who had given him money for this purpose. In 1849 a settlement was made in Utah valley, to the south of the main colony, and in the same year in the Tooele valley, to the southwest. The following year witnessed the settlement of Parowan, in Southern Utah, by George A. Smith, and of the San Bernardino valley, in California, by Amasa M. Lyman and Charles C. Rich. In the first case, that of Parowan, the men were selected according to the needs of a new settlement; in the second, the settlement was made by volunteers — m o r e than five hundred of them. It was not till 1854 that Carson valley, in what is now Nevada, was made into a county by the legislature of Utah.

President Brigham Young

All these settlements were made within the plan of t h e Church authorities to create two lines of settlements to the sea— one from Salt Lake City to Los Angeles and the other f r o m Salt Lake City to San Francisco. So, too, were the settlements in between and along the lines, such as Provo and Nephi, on the way to Los Angeles.

Meanwhile efforts were put forth to organize a political government under the Federal Constitution. The first government was, as we already know, mainly ecclesiastical. There were wards within the Salt Lake stake. But in the year 1849, what came to be known as the State of Deseret was formed, with Brigham Young as governor. It included much more territory than does the Utah of the present time. This was intended to be only a provisional government. What the people of Deseret wanted was statehood. Instead, however, they got a territorial form of government, in 1850—to their great disappointment. Four of the seven appointees were local men. This included Governor Young, who served till 1857, when an outside man was appointed to the office of governor.

Meanwhile, too, the commonwealth progressed in many directions. In 1850 a newspaper, named the *Deseret News*, was established, with Dr. Willard Richards as editor. In 1863 work was begun on the famous Salt Lake Tabernacle. Into it was built what was then the largest pipe organ in the world. This spacious auditorium, with its huge elliptical roof and unusual acoustic properties, was completed in 1867.

The year 1865 saw the extension of a telegraph line through the country, from the east coast to the west coast. In Utah, a name that was given to Deseret at the time the territorial form of government was created, a telegraph line was stretched from the Bear Lake settlements, most of which are now in Idaho, to St. George, in Southern Utah, the work of local interests. This enabled the government in Salt Lake City to keep in communication with all parts of the territory. And then, in 1869, came the railroad, to displace the ox or the mule team as carriers of freight and passengers to Utah.

Such was the material growth of the Mormon colony. The population increased very fast, as one would imagine, and what is more it was on a permanent basis, unlike some other communities in the West, which had a mushroom growth. The Mormons had

come here to make homes, not to make money or to
seek influence or power for the leaders. In 1850 there
were about fifteen thousand persons in the country
now included in Utah. By 1870, however, the population of Utah had jumped to around eighty-seven
thousand. The number now in the state exceeds half
a million. The Mormon people, under the blessings
of heaven, had established a permanent home in a
country of which the American statesman, Daniel
Webster, had said, "What do we want with this vast,
worthless area—this region of savages and wild
beasts, of deserts, of shifting sands and whirlwinds
of dust, of cactus and prairie dogs? To what use could
we ever hope to put those great deserts, or those endless mountain ranges, impenetrable, and covered to
their very base with eternal snow?"

Exactly ten years after the arrival of the pioneers
in the Salt Lake valley, the Utah commonwealth was
stirred by one of the most extraordinary events
in Mormon history. It has been variously called the
Utah Expedition, the Utah War, and the Johnston
Army Episode.

In 1857 the population of Utah was about thirty
thousand. Fully ten thousand of these had come from
England, Scotland, and Wales during the preceding
three years. They had crossed the plains in wagons,
drawn by horses or mules or oxen, and many of them
with pushcarts. In two of the handcart companies
there had been great suffering and loss of life, on account of their late start from the Missouri river. The
inhabitants of Utah at this time were scattered from
Bear Lake on the north to St. George on the south.
There were also Mormon colonies in California, Idaho,
and Nevada.

During the period of the territorial government,
up to 1857, the people here had chafed somewhat over
the fact that all the officials were not local men. Not

only did they deem themselves capable of self-government, but they had had much experience in self-government—on the plains, particularly, and during the
first year in the Salt Lake valley. And it is a notorious
fact that the appointees in a Territory often have
been men who rendered political service only, for
which they were "rewarded" by the party in power.
This appears to have been the case in Utah.

One of the outside officials in Utah, Judge William
W. Drummond, represented to the attorney-general at
Washington that the Mormons had destroyed the
court records, that Federal judges were insulted in
Utah, that the Federal government had been traduced,
that Governor Young had approved the burning of
the court records, and other things to the same effect.
These charges were made in a letter of resignation
by the judge which was written from California,
whither the judge had gone. This letter had been pre-
ceded by one from a former mail contractor to President Buchanan, which was to the same effect. Without
any investigation whatever, the authorities in Washington ordered an army to Utah, to put down a rebellion that did not exist and to install a new governor,
Alfred Cumming, into office. The force was under
the command of Colonel Albert Sidney Johnston, who
later enlisted and fought on the side of the South in
the Civil War.

Had the President investigated, he would have
found out some very interesting things. In the first
place, he would have been led to question the word of
those who had made these serious charges against
the Mormons. Magraw, the ex-mail carrier, had lost
a bid for another contract, because he had been much
higher than a Mormon bidder—which was to the
credit of those who gave the mail contracts; and a
suspicion, at least, might be suggested of a petty
revenge on the part of the disgruntled former mail
carrier. As for Judge Drummond, he had had no

reputation in his home state—Illinois—as a lawyer;
he had deserted a wife and children there, and, picking
up a woman on the streets of Washington, had brought
her to Utah where he introduced her as his wife. Besides, was it at all likely that a people who had raised
five hundred men to fight for their country in the war
with Mexico would become disloyal to their government? The least that the President could have done
was to require Drummond and Magraw to prove their
charges or to face men who denied them. But he did
not do that. Instead he ordered an army, at an excessive cost to the nation, to go out to Utah, to quell
a "rebellion."

Governor Young decided to resist the army.
Several reasons produced this decision. First, he had
had no official notice of his removal, nor of the coming
of the troops. So far as he knew officially, therefore,
he was still governor, and the soldiers approaching the
territory were a foreign force. Second, this army,
whatever its source, appeared to be coming to destroy
the Mormon people, just as other armies in the past
had attempted to do. John Taylor, who had passed
the army on his way from New York to the valley,
stated that the soldiers had boasted about what they
would do to the Mormons when they reached Utah.
This was a time, we must remember, when the Saints
were in disfavor with the nation and a time, too,
when people were much less tolerant. Third, the
Mormon people had done nothing to warrant such
treatment at the hands of the Federal government.
They knew that the action taken by the administration
against them was wholly unwarranted. The charges
were lies, invented and disseminated by corrupt political adventurers and disappointed profiteers.

Accordingly the Mormons armed themselves and
organized to repel the invaders. Men went out into
the mountains and sought in every way to protect

their people. Meantime the troops, twenty-five hundred of them, entered the mountain country, but had
to establish winter quarters about three hundred miles
from Salt Lake City. With the army, as already
stated, was the new governor, with a judge to replace
the unhappy Drummond.

But two friends of the Mormons intervened and
saved the administration and the Saints from further
conflict. These were Captain Stewart Van Vliet and
Colonel Thomas L. Kane. The latter was a particular
friend of the Mormons, and had been for some time.
Kane was also a friend of President Buchanan's.
Conferences were held between these men and the
leaders here, with the result that the army was allowed to enter the valley, provided they only passed
through and encamped off some distance to the
southwest of the city. But President Young did not
trust the soldiers. He called upon the people living in
Salt Lake City and to the north to leave their homes
for some place in the south—just where no one knew.
Moreover, preparations were made to set fire to
whatever would burn in the valley, so that the army,
when it arrived, would find the place as much of a
desert as when the Saints first came here! Later the
troops passed through the city as agreed, the governor
was installed, and the people, as soon as it was certain
that the army had gone, returned to their homes.

The coming of the army to Utah under the circumstances and their stay in the southwestern part
of the valley proved both a blessing and a curse to
the Saints. The army needed provisions, and these
the Mormons furnished at good prices. But morally
the soldiers were a great detriment, often becoming
intoxicated and disorderly, and attracting vice which
the community had done without.

Chapter XVIII

ECONOMIC TEAMWORK IN EARLY UTAH

We have seen that the Prophet planned in Jackson county, Missouri, that every man who stood at the head of a family should work, that, if he did so, he was entitled to whatever was necessary to maintain himself and his dependents in comfort and decency, but that whatever he earned in addition to his needs he was to turn over to the community, to be used for the benefit of the group life.

On the trek westward the motto was, as we have also seen, "If any man shall seek to build up himself, and seeketh not my (the Lord's) counsel, he shall have no power, and his folly shall be made manifest." And the Mormons, as a rule, lived up to this ideal. Few, if any, thought of themselves only. On the contrary, they worked for the good of all. Garden Grove and Mount Pisgah, as already noted, were established through community effort. Once, at the latter place, Charles C. Rich, who was presiding there, was given fifty dollars by a stranger; but the flour which he purchased with this money he distributed among the needy in the community. On another occasion at the same place Lorenzo Snow, one of Elder Rich's counselors, collected several hundred dollars in contributions from well-to-do men in his home state of Ohio, and this money, too, went to help the poor at Mount Pisgah. The same spirit of helpfulness manifested itself in the towns of Kanesville, Council Bluffs, and Winter Quarters, on the Missouri river. And so it was on the way west between the Missouri river and the Salt Lake basin.

On coming to Salt Lake valley, where he expected

to establish a permanent home for his people, Brigham
Young laid down an essential rule. It was that no man
should have any more land than he could take care of.
The water, he said, went with the land. The timber,
too, on the mountains to the east of the valley, was to
belong to no one man or group of men. Moreover,
when that first furrow was plowed in the valley and
potatoes, corn, and other seeds planted, there was
no thought that it was for any particular person.
Nor did each man go off by himself for the purpose
of selecting the best piece of land and cultivating it.
Rather every one waited till after the needs of all
the settlers were satisfied. No land was distributed to
heads of families till after President Young returned
in the fall of 1848. And then, too, a little later, the
big field was plowed and fenced and planted and
harvested mainly through community effort.

*   *   *   *   *

Very early, also, co-operative stores were established throughout the territory, so as to reduce the
cost of merchandise to the people and to keep as much
money at home as was possible under the circumstances.

During the years before there was a railroad in
Utah, goods were brought by trains of wagons, drawn
by mules or oxen. This was, of course, very expensive,
and so prices were high, often exorbitant. Since there
was no competition, to speak of, the merchants charged
as much as "the traffic would bear." Some of these
merchants were Mormons, some were non-Mormons,
but they all made money.

When President Young saw these men piling up
huge fortunes at the expense of the masses, he decided
that something should be done about it. More things
must be made at home. The people must pull together
better. Prices must come down. So he moved along
two lines—home manufactures and co-operation in

buying and selling. He believed that Utah should make most of the things the people needed. Already much had been done in the way of manufacturing. A sugar plant had been established in the southeastern part of Salt Lake City. Planing and flour mills had been built. In Iron county the manufacture of cook-stoves had made a good start. And now what is known as Zion's Co-operative Mercantile Institution (abbreviated to Z C M I) was established.

This was an organization that covered the entire population of the Church in the West. It was not intended only for the people living in Salt Lake City, as is often thought. A "co-op" store was to be set up in every principal town in the territory, with the people there owning the stock, and these were to be fed from the main storehouse in the capital city, or some storehouse centrally located, like Provo and Logan. If there were merchants in any town where it was desirable to establish a "co-op," they were expected to join the larger movement, and, as a matter of fact, nearly all of them did so. The main difficulty experienced in this enterprise was in getting the right kind of management. Men of ability in this line of endeavor were scarce. And then, too, a good many people did not understand and appreciate the move-ment. Hence it did not succeed as well as its organizers had anticipated. But it pointed the way.

*   *   *   *   *

In those days men were called to do particular things. This was, of course, because certain tasks had to be done, and the President of the Church selected the men on whom he could depend to perform these tasks. Thus Erastus Snow was called to settle St. George; George A. Smith, to settle Parowan; Amasa M. Lyman and Charles C. Rich, to establish a settlement in the San Bernardino valley; and Orson Hyde, to colonize Carson valley. And thus, too, in the early fifties, Lorenzo Snow was asked to go to Brigham City, to preside over the settlement there.

Now, President Snow (he became the fifth President of the Church), besides being highly spiritual in his nature, had a very practical bent. He set in motion there a co-operative plan that became known and praised over all the territory and in other parts of the country.

A practical psychologist, President Snow came to the conclusion that people, in order to be happy, needed three things: First, they had to have food to eat, a house to shelter them, and clothes to wear. Second, they must have some sort of recreation, so as to occupy their leisure time. And third, they should have religion, spiritual truth. It was on these three satisfactions that he based what he did in Brigham City. We shall here be concerned only with the material side of that work.

Here is a description by Elder Snow himself of the co-operative plan which he put into operation:

> We commenced over twelve years ago (this was said in 1876) by organizing a mercantile department, which consisted of four stockholders, myself included, with a capital of about three thousand dollars. As this enterprise prospered, we continued to receive capital stock, also adding new names to the list of stockholders, and succeeded in uniting the interests of the people and securing their patronage. We resolved then to commence home industries and receive our dividends, if any, in the articles produced.
>
> It required some efforts to reconcile their feelings with a knowledge of their duty and obligations as elders of Israel and servants of God. A good spirit, however, prevailed, and a desire to build up the kingdom of God, and work for the interests of the people outweighed all selfish considerations.
>
> We erected a tannery building, with modern improvements and conveniences, at a cost of $10,000. Most of the materials and work was furnished as capital stock by such persons as desired an interest in the institution. The larger portion of this work was done in the winter season, when no employment could be had. Thus we gained twenty or thirty

new stockholders. This tannery has been in operation during the past nine years, with success and reasonable profits, producing an excellent quality of leather, from $8,000 to $10,000 annually. We connected with this branch of industry a boot and shoe shop; also a saddle and harness shop.

Our next enterprise was a woolen factory. During the past seven years this factory has done a satisfactory business. With the view to getting wool we now started a sheep herd, commencing with fifteen hundred head. They now number five thousand. Our next business was the establishment of a dairy. Having selected a suitable ranch, we commenced with sixty cows, erected some temporary buildings, bought some machinery, and now it is the best and most commodious dairy in this Territory, producing each season in the neighborhood of $8,000 in butter and cheese. Next we started a horn stock herd, numbering at present one thousand, which supplies, in connection with the sheep herd, a meat market, owned by our association. Also we have a hat factory, in which we produce all our fur and wool hats. We make our own tinware—have a pottery, broom, brush, and molasses factory, a shingle mill and two saw mills, operated by water power, and one steam mill; and also blacksmith, tailor, and furniture departments, and one for putting up and repairing wagons and carriages. We have established a cotton farm of one hundred and twenty-five acres in the southern part of the Territory, for the purpose of supplying warps to our woolen factory, where we maintain a colony of about twenty young men. We have a department for manufacturing straw hats, in which we employ from fifteen to twenty girls.

As this institution expanded, other stockholders came in, giving work in exchange for stock, till presently practically every one in Brigham City was a member of the association. And all the stockholders took their dividends in the articles produced by the numerous departments of the organization. In the main, too, as stated by its chief organizer, the work was done during slack seasons on the farm. Ready cash was not much to be had in those days.

* * * * *

Before President Young died, in 1877, however, he began the establishment of the United Order, in various phases, in the commonwealth.

At a general conference of the Church, in 1874, President Young announced as the theme the "United

Order of Brotherhood." And he asked those who might be called upon to speak on the occasion to give their views on the subject. Among the speakers at this conference was President George A. Smith, a counselor in the First Presidency. "A United Order," he said, "would organize a community so that all the ingenuity, talent, skill, and energy it possessed would inure to the good of the whole. This is the object and design in the establishment of these organizations. It is perfectly certain that there is in every community a sufficient amount of energy and skill and labor to supply all its wants, and put all its members in possession of every necessary and comfort of life—if this skill and energy be rightly directed." Other speakers similarly indorsed the movement.

Following this conference the apostles went out into the commonwealth, to preach the movement and to organize it wherever they found the people prepared for it. Elders Wilford Woodruff and Charles C. Rich went to the Bear Lake valley, where they organized co-operatives. In these the people generally had stock. There was private ownership, as elsewhere, but factories and stores and other public enterprises were community owned. The plan here was to manufacture whatever the people needed in the way of food and clothing. This was not exactly the United Order, but it was a brotherhood—which is the underlying idea of the Order.

In other communities they "had all things common," as was the case, it seems, in the early Christian church. The Order was established in some settlements on the Little Colorado. These being, for the most part, small communities, the people all ate at the same table, although they had separate homes and farms, and they worked the land collectively. At Sunset there were but twenty-five families—twenty-four men, thirty women, and sixty-six children. Thirteen of the men worked on the farms. At the table each man, with his family, had a designated place, and the food was cooked jointly by the women. As long as this order of things continued, there was general satisfaction with the plan. Of course, otherwise the regular organizations of the Church prevailed—stakes, wards, and auxiliary societies.

In still other communities, there was the United Order as Joseph Smith designed it. This was particularly the case in what is now Sevier County, Utah. That is, there was private ownership of homes and the implements of production, whatever they might be, and each head of a family deducted from what he earned the amount necessary for his needs. All else was publicly owned. Houses were built through community effort; groceries were delivered by men in the employ of the community; each man was assigned to the work for which he was best fitted. Surplus goods were disposed of to Salt Lake City residents, which brought in some cash. This cash was expended to purchase more land and to make improvements.

These experiments in the economic life were brought to an end during the administration of President John Taylor. The reason lay in the fact that some of them did not come up to the expectations of the Church leaders, who thought it best to abandon them all.

* * * * *

In later periods of the Church in the West, too, there has been a good deal of teamwork economically, but in a different form and on a smaller scale.

Where settlements by Latter-day Saints were unable to finance the digging of canals, for instance, the Church, to the extent that it was able to do so, came to the rescue, especially if the community showed prospects of growing beyond the point where a small canal would serve. Such aid and guidance have been rendered by the Church, not only in Utah, but also in Idaho, Wyoming, and other states.

The Church has encouraged the building of factories, too, and the establishment of industries. A notable example of this is the beet sugar industry in Utah and Idaho. President Woodruff took the initiative here. He was determined that sugar should be manufactured by his people. He wished, for one thing, to provide a means of income for the farmers and, for another thing, to make the commonwealth more nearly self-supporting.

As a result of his determination and of financial help from the Church, a factory was established in Lehi, a small town a few miles south of Salt Lake City, and the manufacture of sugar was begun. This factory was established in 1891, although attempts had been made to produce sugar during the administrations of Brigham Young and John Taylor. Before his elevation to the presidency of the Church Wilford Woodruff had been head of the Agricultural and Manufacturing Society for twenty-five years—which accounts in part for his keen interest in farmers and producers generally.

Chapter XIX

SPIRITUAL ACTIVITIES

One would think that in the whirlpool of materiality in which Mormonism was now overwhelmed there would be little thought given to spiritual matters. That, however, was far from the case. And this is one of the notable things about the Church.

The truth is that the Mormon leaders have been deeply concerned about carrying the new movement into all parts of the earth. To Joseph Smith and his followers was repeated the commission given to the ancient apostles to go "into all the world and preach the gospel to every creature, acting in the authority which I have given you." They were to proclaim chiefly the doctrine of repentance wherever they went. And so, no matter what the conditions otherwise in which the Saints found themselves, the leaders of the Church were always conscious of the duty imposed upon them to carry or send the message of the restored gospel to mankind everywhere.

Instances during the administration of the Prophet will illustrate the way in which this obligation was carried on.

When, in 1837, he was surrounded by men who even sought his life and when men he had trusted were falling away from the faith, he sent two of the apostles, with others, to England, to proclaim the Word there. We have spoken of this mission in another place. Elders Heber C. Kimball and Orson Hyde, with Elder Willard Richards and Elder Joseph Fielding, began missionary work in England which has flourished ever since; more than a hundred thousand converts have been made in the British Isles.

Again, in 1839, when an even worse lot had befallen the Saints, eight of the apostles, with a few other elders, went on a mission to Great Britain. This was after the Mormons had been expelled from Missouri and after they had begun to establish themselves in what was to become Nauvoo. On this mission, as we have seen, some five thousand people joined the Church, a collection of hymns was published, an English edition of the *Book of Mormon* was put out, and a periodical issued, *The Millennial Star*. It would almost seem that when the fortunes of the Mormons were at the lowest ebb, a mission was projected which more than made up for any misfortune that may have overtaken them.

And now, once more, when a great calamity, as it appeared, had come upon the new movement and they were struggling to recuperate their strength in a new home under untried conditions, the organization put forth its greatest effort to carry the message of the restored gospel to various nations—some of which had never before been visited by Mormon missionaries. And as a result of this effort tens of thousands of men and women in these nations took up the banner of Mormonism, and thousands of them immigrated to the Great West, where the new movement had set up its ensign.

*   *   *   *

Before the Prophet's death, four men were called on a mission to the Pacific Islands. They were Addison Pratt, Noah Rogers, Benjamin F. Grouard, and Knowlton Hanks.

Whether or not President Smith regarded the Islanders as related in any way to the American natives, is not known. The *Book of Mormon* tells of a certain Hagoth who launced forth "into the west sea" and was "never heard of more." Many Mormons, among them the late George Q. Cannon, have believed

the inhabitants of the Pacific Islands to be related
to the American Indians, and this view is shared by
non-Mormon students of the subject. For anything
we know to the contrary, their origin may be traced
to the expedition made by this Nephite Hagoth.

Leaving New Bedford, Massachusetts, in May,
1843, three of these missionaries landed on the island
of Tubual, of the Austral group, one year later.
(Elder Hanks had died at sea.) Later the missionaries established headquarters at Tahiti, in the Society
Islands. In July, 1845, Elder Rogers returned to
Nauvoo, after circumnavigating the globe. Elder
Pratt, in the early part of 1847, left the islands and
went to Salt Lake City, whither his people had mi-
grated in the meantime. He had been gone at his
own expense for about four years, and, with Elders
Rogers and Grouard, had baptized twelve hundred
natives and whites.

The Sandwich Islands, now known as the
Hawaiian Islands, received visits from Mormon elders
in the year 1850. There were ten missionaries in all—
Hiram Clark, Thomas Whittle, Henry W. Bigler,
Thomas Morris, John Dixon, William Farrer, James
Hawkins, Hiram Blackwell, James Keeler, and
George Q. Cannon. They arrived at Honolulu in
December, 1850. They had left their homes in Salt
Lake City in the midsummer of 1849.

The story of that mission is extremely interesting. Here, however, we can give only the barest out-
line. The missionaries, it seems, were expected to
preach only to the whites there. But these were not
interested. Then the question arose as to whether the
elders should not take the gospel to the natives. Of
the ten men in the mission five of them were for going
home; the other five decided to remain. The leader
of the elders who wished to remain was George Q.
Cannon, who was to serve for many years in the First
Presidency of the Church. Elder Cannon had received
a manifestation from the Lord that he should con-

tinue his mission on the islands and preach to the natives, who would receive his message. He was enabled by the gift of the Holy Spirit to learn the language in an incredibly short time. This group of five missionaries remained on the islands till 1854. Later Elder Joseph F. Smith, then a boy of fifteen, served as a missionary on the same group of islands.

At the October general conference of the Church, held in Salt Lake City, in 1849, the apostle John Taylor, with Curtis E. Bolton and John Pack, was called on a mission to France; the apostle Erastus Snow, with Peter O. Hansen and John E. Forsgren, to Scandinavia; the apostle Lorenzo Snow, with Joseph Toronto, to Italy. Thirteen days later the company— which included the apostle Franklin D. Richards and others, who were going to Great Britain—was on its way to the Atlantic seaboard in twelve wagons, we are told, drawn by forty-two horses and mules. At this same general conference the apostles Amasa M. Lyman and Charles C. Rich were appointed to a mission in California, and Addison Pratt and James S. Brown to the Society Islands.

When the apostle Taylor arrived in France, in July, 1850, he found that the mission had already been opened by William Howell, a Welsh convert, who had been a Baptist minister. Elder Howell had been appointed to the French mission at a conference of the Church in Manchester, in August, 1849, and had gone at once to Havre. Here he had called on many of the clergy, both French and English; had visited English families there; and had even gone on board some ships outward bound, to deliver the message of Mormonism to passengers and crew. Also he had given four hundred French tracts to William C. Dunbar, who was a missionary in Jersey, to distribute among the people on that island. Then he had gone to Jersey, at Elder Dunbar's request, to aid in the work there. Elder Howell told the readers of the *Millennial Star* that the money to finance this mission was coming from "the little my wife gains in business, which, to save a clerk's salary, she attends herself, occasionally until the midnight hours." There were many baptisms, too, particularly in Jersey. One of the converts here was Philip De La Mare, a young man of twenty-six, and well-to-do. Later he was to be a large contributor to the building of the first sugar factory in Utah, and its manager.

Soon after the arrival in Boulogne-sur-mer of the missionaries from America, we find six elders in France. Of these, however, only Elder Bolton could speak the language. "Our principal aim," Elder Taylor explained in the *Star*, "is to get some one into the Church who can preach it (Mormonism), and set them to work." One of the first converts in Boulogne was a journalist of great ability, named Louis A. Bertrand, who did much useful service in a literary way. After the departure of Elder Taylor to Utah, Elder Bertrand was made counselor to Elder Bolton, and in 1861, after he had gone to Utah himself, he was called to preside over the French mission. Believing that the Mormons should represent themselves in order to avoid being misrepresented by others, the apostle Taylor, with the help of Elder Bolton and Elder Bertrand, had the *Book of Mormon* translated into French and published, the translation having been done by Elder Bolton. Then President Taylor established the *Etoile du Deseret*, which, however, continued only one year. Also he wote numerous articles for the French newspapers, and many of these were published. Meantime baptisms were performed at Boulogne, at Havre, in Paris, and, as already noted, on the island of Jersey.

Toward the end of his mission Elder Taylor became interested in the sugar industry in France. He wished to see the industry introduced in Utah. At Arras an old convent, Elder Bolton tells us, had been turned into a sugar factory, and the two missionaries spent much of their time there. On a trip to England the apostle had succeeded in getting a subscription of five thousand dollars from a Mr. Collins, a wealthy manufacturer, an equal amount from a Mr. Coward. a dealer in salt, and forty-five thousand dollars from Captain Russel, a Scottish shipbuilder—all Mormon converts. A company was formed, with De La Mare in charge, and a sugar factory was built in what is now known as Sugar House, a suburb of Salt Lake City.

*   *   *   *   *

While the German mission did not really grow out of the French mission, yet it was closely connected with it in its beginnings.

In 1842 the apostle Orson Hyde visited Germany, and actually published a periodical there—*Zion's Panier*, a monthly. This was at Hamburg. But we hear nothing more of the missionary work in Germany till September, 1851, when George P. Dykes, fleeing from opposition in Denmark, went there. After preaching Mormonism in Schleswig for some time, he baptized two persons "in the same waters," Elder Dykes assures us, "where the first Christians were baptized." In October of this year (1851) the apostle Taylor went to Germany from France. Elder Dykes, who had assisted Elder Snow in the opening of the Scandinavian mission, now turned his hand to assist Elder Taylor in Germany. There the two established again the periodical begun by Elder Hyde, and commenced the translation of the *Book of Mormon* into German. In 1852 we find a church in Hamburg of thirty members. Later other elders came into the field to do missionary work—George C. Riser, Jacob Secrist, and George Sayer. Orson Spencer, president of the European mission at the time, paid a visit to Germany.

There was much opposition, however. Meetings

were held only in private homes. The officials were always on the alert for political agitators, among whom they erroneously counted the Mormon missionaries. Once, Elder Riser tells us, he was taken by the officers into a room "with iron curtains," where he spent some time "with the Bible."

One of the early converts in Germany was the late educator, Karl G. Maeser, who for many years was to be connected with Utah schools and with the Brigham Young Academy, now the Brigham Young University. Born in Meissen, he was converted in Dresden, where he taught school. One dark night, just after his baptism, he and President Franklin D. Richards, with William Budge, were walking home. Dr. Maeser and the President were conversing, Elder Budge acting as interpreter. Said President Richards to his fellow American, "You don't need to interpret any longer; Brother Maeser and I understand each other perfectly." It was the gift of tongues, in answer to Dr. Maeser's prayer, on coming out of the water, that he might have "some manifestation from heaven" concerning the new movement. Dr. Maeser spoke in German and President Richards in English. On embracing Mormonism Dr. Maeser resigned his position as head teacher in the Budig Institute and went to England, where he labored as a missionary among the German residents of London, before going to America.

* * * * *

The apostle Erastus Snow, with Elders Hansen and Forsgren, went directly to Copenhagen, Denmark, where he established headquarters. Elder Forsgren at first labored in Sweden, where he was born. It was there that the first baptism in Scandinavia was performed by a Mormon elder. The elder had converted his brother. This was in 1850. Elder Hansen worked in Denmark. A new missionary—Hans F.

Peterson—went to Norway, to preach the gospel. Thus the whole of Scandinavia was visited by the missionaries.

Presently the *Book of Mormon* was translated into Danish, and published. This was in 1851. Also a periodical—the *Stjerne*—was established. All this labor, however, was not accomplished without opposition in all three countries. At Alborg, where there was a branch of the Church, the assembly hall in which the Saints met for religious services, was destroyed by a mob. Elder Dykes, as we have seen, was forced to leave Denmark, and Elder Forsgren was arrested and banished from Sweden—although not long afterward he converted some of those who had brought about his banishment.

The labors of these and other missionaries, however, was rewarded by many baptisms. Here are some figures of conversions in Scandinavia during the years indicated:

1850	139
1851	555
1852	992
1853	2,052
1854	2,483
1855	2,692
1858	3,709

* * * * *

Elder Lorenzo Snow, with Joseph Toronto and T. B. H. Stenhouse, went first to Genoa, Italy, and then to the valley of Piedmont. Elder Stenhouse had been working in England as a missionary for the Church, where he was president of the Southampton conference. Later Jabez Woodard, also an English missionary, joined the Italian mission. These two men were not only educated, but they had a literary talent that aided greatly in putting the gospel before the Italian people. The apostle Snow presently made Elder Woodard president of the Italian mission and

Elder Stenhouse president of the Swiss mission. Only
Elder Toronto, who was born in Sardinia and who was
now sent there to preach, was able to speak the
language.

Soon after the arrival of the missionaries in
Italy Elder Snow wrote some pamphlets, which,
through the influence of Elder Orson Pratt, were
translated by a professor in the College of Paris.
Elder Pratt was then president of the British mission.
In Switzerland Elder Stenhouse began the publication
of a periodical—*The Reflector*. In 1852 a translation
of the *Book of Mormon* was finished and published
in the Italian language. Also steps were taken to
create an organization of the Church in Piedmont.

By this time an Englishman, an Italian, a Scot,
and a Welshman had been baptized. So the first
organization, as the apostle Snow truly says, comprised men from four different nations! A letter to
the *Millennial Star*, in England, stated that there
were thirty members of the Church in Italy and one
hundred forty in Switzerland. Among those in Piedmont who were baptized were the Malan family.
"Several intelligent and influential Italians," President Snow wrote to the *Star*, "have lately been
ordained to the priesthood, and are now engaged in
propagating the principles of life and salvation."
Later some forty more baptisms were performed in
Italian cities.

Here is the testimony of an eighty-year-old convert in Basel, Switzerland: "After having received
baptism and the imposition of hands, I have experienced within me a regeneration before unknown—
peace, accompanied with joy, which has nothing of
an earthly nature; something exclusively spiritual,
accompanied with a determination to conform to the
gospel my thoughts, my words, and my conduct."

And thus it went. The gospel message was

carried, not only to the islands of the Pacific, to France and Germany, to Italy, to Switzerland, and to the Scandinavian countries, but also to Holland, to Austria, and later to India, and later still to Japan. In England alone, with Ireland, Wales, and Scotland, during these first years, tweny-two thousand persons were baptized, and the subscription of the *Star* was increased to seven times what it had been.

Chapter XX

ANOTHER PERIOD OF CONFLICT

When the Latter-day Saints came to what is now known at Utah, the country was an uninhabited desert. We have seen what Senator Webster said of it—shifting sands, deep snows, a worthless area. That was not far from the truth. The only inhabitants in the entire West of that period were Indians, trappers, and Catholic missionaries. And the Mormons settled in the heart of this solitude.

In order, therefore, to survive, the Saints would have to raise everything they needed to eat and most of what they required for clothing. And they acted on this assumption. It has already been stated that, as soon as the first company entered the Salt Lake valley, they began to plow and to plant. Although, as we have seen, the first winter in the mountain home was mild, there was a shortage of food the following year, on account of the crickets. Crickets and grasshoppers were to visit the commonwealth in other years—notably in the year 1867, when grasshoppers covered the streets of Salt Lake City to the depth of an inch or more. Food stuffs, however, were produced in various parts of the new home, and so there was no suffering.

As soon as possible, too, manufacturing was begun. Very early grist mills and saw mills were set up. In the early fifties the making of sugar was attempted, but with little success at first. Responding to the advice of President Young, "Let home industry produce every article of home consumption," laws were passed by the territorial legislature to encourage manufacturing. Cotton was grown in southern Utah, which with wool from sheep that had been brought here, was made into dresses and suits. A paper mill was set up in a canyon running into the Salt Lake valley. In Iron county stoves were made. Even silk culture was established. And when gold was discovered in California, paper money, with gold dust in reserve, was made here, to facilitate the exchange of goods. Brigham Young helped to set the type for the printing of the money.

One of the first things the pioneers did was to induce the Federal government to establish a mail route between Salt Lake City and the East. In 1852 the legislature of the territory petitioned for a telegraph line. This did not come, however, till the administration of Lincoln. Presently the Deseret Telegraph line was extended north and south through the territory—from the Bear Lake valley to St. George. It was not till 1869 that the railroad entered Utah. The line followed by the railroad from the Missouri river to the Rocky Mountains was, in the main, that made by the Mormons on their way west. Up to that time freight came to Utah in wagons, drawn by mules or oxen. In consequence merchandise was high-priced.

With food stuffs, produced through irrigation; with manufacturing on an increasingly large scale; with the transportation of news and merchandise from the East to the West at a comparatively fast rate. Utah was on its way to the same sort of material prosperity that other parts of the country enjoyed.

Nor did the Mormons neglect the higher life. Most of them had the educational advantages of the communities from which they had come. Illiteracy has always been low in Utah. No sooner had the first company of Saints arrived in the valley of the Salt Lake than they set up a school in a tent. A little later they established what is now known as the University of Utah—the first college west of the Missouri. Its first president—Orson Spencer—had a master's degree. Its professor of mathematics was Orson Pratt, a man with an international reputation. In 1852 a library was established. The Congress, at the suggestion of Dr. John M. Bernhisel, delegate from Utah, had appropriated five thousand dollars for this purpose. Two years earlier a newspaper— *The Deseret News*—had been issued, with Dr. Willard Richards as editor. Social Hall, in Salt Lake City, was dedicated on the first day of the year 1853. Nine years later the Deseret Dramatic Association gave the first performance in the Salt Lake Theater, which was then and for many years afterward one of the best playhouses in the nation.

Such was the way in which the Mormon people overcame the elemental struggle for a life of safety and culture in the new home—a struggle to get food, clothing, and shelter from the weather, a struggle, too, with the downward pull of frontier conditions.

* * * * *

Indian difficulties were not so common among the Mormons as among other Americans in the West. This was due mainly to the beliefs of the Latter-day Saints concerning the American natives. These Lamanites, as the Mormons came to call them, were descendants of the peoples spoken of in the *Book of Mormon*. They had a great future as well as a notable past, as the Saints believed. While it was the custom elsewhere to treat the Indian as if he were a wild animal, in the Mormon communities he was accorded the same treatment as other human beings. "It is better," said Brigham Young, "to feed than to fight the Indian." At the same time he advised the people to keep their distance, and not be too familiar with the natives. Also he sent such men as Jacob Hamblin to teach them agriculture and industry. The Saints never lied to the Indians, nor attempted to take advantage of them in any way. The result was that, in the native mind, the white man was one of two classes—"Americans" and "Mormons." And he acted accordingly toward them.

As soon as the pioneers entered the Salt Lake basin they were visited by some Indians, who were inspired by curiosity mainly. They showed no particular unfriendliness toward the new comers, but no doubt they were more or less surprised and disappointed that their hunting grounds should be invaded by such a large group of whites.

Had all persons in Utah minded their own business, as they had been urged to do, almost no trouble would have been experienced with the natives. In one place, for instance, two men, non-Mormons, killed three young Indians, for taking a calf in the winter time when they were extremely hungry. Another native was wounded, but succeeded in reaching his tribe. The result was that there was an Indian uprising against the whites. On another occasion a company of whites on their way to the west coast shot a native, who was entirely innocent of any harm. There was another uprising. Where the Indians were let alone by the whites, they usually proved peaceful. In Bear Lake valley, for instance, the leader of the colony there—the apostle Charles C. Rich—made a pact with the native tribes respecting the occupancy of the land there. In consequence the colonists in that valley had no difficulty with the natives.

Still in spite of the care with which the Mormon leaders treated the Indians, there were serious disagreements. The natives sometimes proved intractable. In Provo, in the year 1849, the fort there would probably have been wiped out by Indians, had not Charles C. Rich, a man of great tact, happened along and conciliated the natives. Later in Utah and Sanpete counties there were attacks by Indians. On the whole, however, the Mormons got along with the natives much better than any other western commu-

nity, and they were complimented on this by the
authorities in Washington.

*   *   *   *   *

Besides a struggle with the Indians and for the
means of subsistence, the early settlers of Utah had
a confict with non-Mormons who followed them into
the Rocky Mountains; only it was somewhat different
from the clashes which they had in their eastern
homes.   •

It was only natural that men and women not
members of the Church should be found in the
Mormon commonwealth. Salt Lake valley, like ancient
Palestine, was on a main highway. In order to reach
the west coast from the eastern states traffic usually
passed through the city of the Saints. Many travelers
remained in Utah, either because they were converted
to the Faith or because they thought to enter business
among the Mormons. Moreover, in the sixties Colonel
Patrick E. Connor, an army officer, was stationed in
the territory, with soldiers, for the purpose, as some
thought, of watching the Mormons. It was at this
time that Fort Douglas was established on the hill to
the east of the city. This, too, drew non-Mormons to
Utah. And so it happened that the population of the
territory became more and more mixed as to religious persuasion. Ordinarily this should not have been
a source of trouble, but in Utah at this time certain
conditions brought on a conflict.

First of all, the leading and most influential man
in the commonwealth took the stand that agriculture
rather than mining should be the occupation of the
people for the present. There can be no doubt that
this position was sound under the circumstances. As
President Young pointed out, people must have food
before anything else. They could not eat gold. Besides,
an agricultural commonwealth was more stable than
any other, especially if it engaged also in manufac-

tures. And then, too, there was always the tempta-
tion, when one got sudden wealth, to forsake God
for Mammon.

A group of men, mainly non-Mormons, took
offense at this position on the part of the President.
They were led by Colonel Connor. It was an attempt,
they said, to "dictate" the policy of the territorial
government. The fact is that President Young was
only giving advice and counsel. There was no doubt
that most of those in Utah would follow this advice,
for they believed in him as their leader. Nevertheless,
this proved a source of conflict in Utah.

Secondly, there was always an undercurrent of ill
feeling between the Saints and some of the Federal
officials in the territory. These officials were often
deeply prejudiced against the Mormons and Mormonism, and they expressed this prejudice on every
possible occasion. What right had Judge Brocchus
or Judge Drummond or Governor Shaffer or Justice
McKean to expect anything but conflict from people
whom they openly insulted and opposed? Brocchus
as much as told the women of Mormondom that they
were unchaste. Shaffer was determined to put President Young in jail, even if he had to wrest the law
in doing so. And McKean went to Utah with the
boast on his lips that his "mission" was to "destroy
Mormonism."

Another source of disagreement lay in the political situation in Utah.

From the first the Mormon people wanted statehood. They believed that, with their experience and
training in self-government, they could take care of
themselves. And such observers as Colonel Thomas L.
Kane thought so, too. The simple truth is that in the
Mormon commonwealth there were many men who
were far abler than those whom the President sent out
to the territory. But time and again the petition of

the Saints was rejected by the national authorities.
It was not till Utah had been settled for fifty years
that this boon was granted its inhabitants.   Their
efforts, as a matter of fact, were frustrated usually
by politicians in the territory. And these gave various
reasons. The Mormons, for one thing, they said, would
set up a theocracy in Utah. Besides, they practiced
polygamy, which ran counter to the monogamic ideal
of the nation and of the world.

It was this last point which, as we shall see
presently, these politicians stressed in their campaign
against the Mormons. Obviously the nation could more
easily be aroused over a moral than over a political
question. And this proved to be the case. They
appealed for anti-polygamy laws, which the Congress
readily granted, and these laws, as we shall see in
another chapter, were applied with a harshness that
was entirely uncalled for.

As a result of almost constant agitation on the
part of disgruntled politicians, mostly in Utah, there
appeared in all sections of the country and in foreign
nations a great deal of opposition to everything Mormon. Stories were fabricated by preachers, politicians, and writers, the purpose of which was to dis-
credit the Mormon people. Mobbings of missionaries
were not uncommon, both in America and in England.
Indeed, some missionaries were murdered outright
in consequence. In the southern states three missionaries were killed by mobs.

* * * * *

In 1877 President Brigham Young passed away
at the age of seventy-six. He had led the Church for
thirty years, not counting the years when the quorum
of Twelve was in charge. His administration had been
marked by energy, wisdom and devotion to the Cause.
As he had promised to do on the death of the Prophet,
he had built upon the foundation laid by Joseph Smith.

During his administration, too, the message of Mormonism had gone to many peoples who had not before heard of it. And then, too, colonization had been pushed out into California and Idaho, Arizona and New Mexico, as well as into all parts of the Territory of Utah.

It is almost universally admitted today that Brigham Young was one of America's great men and her ablest colonizer.

Chapter XXI

LOVE, MARRIAGE, AND HOME

All down the years Mormonism has had as a major interest the home life of its members. It has concerned itself with the relations of husband and wife, children and parents. Mormon views on the subject have undergone no change, although the application of these views may have done so, through the threatened break-down of family ties and the "emancipation of woman" in the principal nations of the world.

As we have seen, Mormonism accepts in a very literal sense the idea that God is "our Father." That is, it teaches that he is the Father of our spirits, not the Creator of them. In other words, it assures us that men are begotten sons, and women the begotten daughters, of God in the spirit. The idea of creation in the sense of bringing into being something out of nothing, is inconsistent with the notion of the Fatherhood of God. To the Latter-day Saints "our Father which art in heaven" has a very real meaning. But Mormonism goes a step farther than any other Christian church. It assumes that we have a Mother in heaven, as well as a Father. "In the Heavens are parents single?" asks one of the favorite Mormon hymns, and answers, "No; the thought makes reason stare!" The words "father" and "mother" are correlative terms; each implies the other.

The theological conception of a Mother in heaven as well as a Father lends dignity to motherhood and wifehood. Joseph Smith was in full agreement with the apostle Paul, who said, "Neither is the man without the woman, neither the woman without the man, in the Lord." And so Mormonism puts woman by the side of man in the scheme of salvation.

* * * * *

"Marriage," declares a revelation to the Prophet, "is ordained of God unto man . . . that the earth might answer the end of its creation and that it might be filled with the measure of man, according to his creation before the world was made." Moreover, marriage is a covenant, a "new and an everlasting covenant," involving the parties to the marriage contract, on the one side, and the Lord, on the other. Thus marriage becomes a matter of the spirit, not merely of the flesh. It is this spiritual basis that gives color and condition to the marriage ceremony among the Mormons.

Very naturally, therefore, the marriage contract is eternal. It is literally "an everlasting covenant." That is, it continues and is "of force" in the next world, not merely in this life. For the Saints interpret the statement attributed to Christ, that "in the resurrection they neither marry nor are given in marriage," to mean merely that the marriage covenant must be entered into in connection with this life, not that there is no recognition of family ties in the hereafter.

Says the revelation: "If a man marry a wife by my word, which is my law, and by the new and everlasting covenant, and it is sealed unto them by the Holy Spirit of promise, by him who is anointed . . . ye shall come forth in the first resurrection; and if it be after the first resurrection, in the next resurrection; and shall inherit thrones, kingdoms, principalities, and powers, dominions, all heights and depths."

* * * * *

The Mormon idea of the family grows out of the idea of the preciousness of the human personality. It cannot too often be repeated that the Saints look on

man as a spirit, and on the spirit as eternal. Physical
bodies are necessary to human progress—the union of
spirit and element. Always, therefore, spirits have
been waiting in the pre-earth world, to acquire bodies
through the process of birth. Hence it is the "duty" of
every normal man and woman to marry and to have
children. Only thus can "the end of creation be answered." The Church, therefore, has always frowned
upon everything that tends to interfere in any way
with the formation and development of the home—
celibacy, late marriage, abortion, fornication, adultery,
divorce, artificial restriction of the number of children in the home, prostitution. And, on the contrary,
it has always encouraged early marriage, home-owner-
ship, freedom from debt, financial independence, large
families, and the establishment of schools, colleges, and
universities.

This doctrine of the eternity of the marriage
covenant was first taught by Joseph Smith in Nauvoo.
Husband and wife were "sealed" to each other. That
is, they were married to each other for eternity as well
as for time, by the president of the Church or by
some one appointed by him. It is so today in the
Church. Every husband and wife, therefore, who
have been united in marriage in this manner look forward to a reunion, with their children, in the next
world. Just as love is "the greatest thing in the world"
of the flesh, so it will be in the world of the spirit. In
other words, family ties will persist in the hereafter,
only more intensified.

Statistics reveal an interesting sidelight on the
efficacy of such marriage. Of divorces in the Mormon
church there were in the year 1934, for instance, 7.6
per thousand, as compared with 14.9 in the United
States.

*   *   *   *   *

In the year 1852 what has come to be known
among the Mormon people as the doctrine of "plural
marriage," commonly known as polygamy, was pub-

licly announced in Utah by the Church authorities, as part of its teachings. The matter is taken up here because of its historical importance. Besides, the doctrine has been so much misunderstood, not to say misrepresented, that the reader should be informed of the true situation.

In 1842 the Prophet entered upon the practice of the principle of plural marriage. So, too, did most of the other leading authorities of the Church, at his request. It was a commandment to him and to them. But the practice of this system of marriage was not so public as at a later time in Utah. It is to be noted, however, that the revelation on the subject is mainly on "celestial marriage," and plural marriage is but a part of celestial marriage. Celestial marriage, as understood by its advocates, is marriage for "time and eternity," just explained.

There is no evidence whatever that plural marriage was practiced by leading Mormons, either in Joseph Smith's time or later in the Utah period, because of lustful desires in them. Bernard Shaw doubtless spoke the truth when he said, the other year, that Joseph Smith would have been deserted by his people if he had advocated a life of licentiousness. At the time the principle was first practiced, both in the Prophet's lifetime and in the early years of Utah, there were no laws in the country against polygamy.

Mormon polygamy was radically different from that to be found in oriental countries. Moreover, with the Saints each wife, with her children, occupied a separate house, or, if the wives lived in the same house, as was sometimes the case, in separate quarters. No distinction was made between either of the wives or the children. The husband provided for each family, was responsible for the education of all the children, and gave both the children and their mothers the same advantages he would have given to his family under the monogamous relationship. If it was thought he could not do this, he was not permitted to enter upon the practice of plural marriage.

There is not space here to discuss the fruits of plural marriage as practiced in early Mormondom, but indications point to the fact that, as a rule, polygamous children were superior physically and mentally to the general run of monogamous children. At best, however, less than three percent of the men in the Church practiced plural marriage.

*   *   *   *   *

Both the theory and practice of plural marriage, especially the practice, provoked fierce opposition, not only in Utah, where it was practiced openly, but in Nauvoo where the practice was more or less secret. Whenever political difficulties arose in Utah, the polygamous practices of the Mormons were bound to be brought into the picture—chiefly to arouse the nation against the Latter-day Saints.

Agitation of the question of Mormon polygamy began as early as 1851, before it had been publicly announced by Brigham Young. It was known, of course, that the Saints had begun the practice of the principle in Nauvoo, Illinois. This is what Judge Brocchus meant when he advised the Mormon women to become "virtuous." In 1860 the Republican Party took cognizance of the question by declaring itself against "slavery and polygamy—twin relics of barbarism." Lincoln, when asked what he was going to do about the Mormons, replied, "I propose to let them alone." And he compared the Utah question to a green hemlock on a frontier farm—it was too heavy to move, and too knotty to split, too wet to burn, but it could be plowed round. And that is what he did—mostly. But in 1862 the Congress of the United States passed an anti-polygamy law, under which it was hoped by the nation to put a stop to plural marriage. The law, however, aimed at plural *marriages*, not polygamous *relations*. The Mormons considered it unconstitutional, as did many non-Mormons throughout the country.

In 1872 the Congress passed, and the president signed, a bill prohibiting polygamy. A test case was brought into the courts of Utah. The Supreme Court of the United States, when the case came up before that body, decided it to be constitutional, and George Reynolds, private secretary to President Young and the principal in the case, was incarcerated, first in the Federal prison in Nebraska and then in the Utah penitentiary. This was the first instance where a man was imprisoned for a polygamous relationship.

Ten years later—that is, in 1882—the Edmunds-Tucker Anti-polygamy Act became law. This, too, the Mormons contested as unconstitutional. It was, they urged, an interference with religious liberty in the United States. On being taken to the Supreme Court, however, the decision of the lower court was upheld. And so the Saints yielded, but not before scores of their most prominent men had served terms in the penitentiary for having more wives than one.

In September, 1890, Wilford Woodruff, who was then president of the Church, issued what was called a "manifesto," in which he publicly declared that "my advice to the Latter-day Saints is to refrain from contracting any marriages forbidden by the law of the land." And in 1896, when Utah became a state, the framers of the Constitution inserted in that document a clause forever prohibiting the practice of polygamy, or plural marriage. This brought to an end an important chapter in the history of the Church.

Chapter XXII

THE ADMINISTRATION OF JOHN TAYLOR

Three years after the death of Brigham Young, John Taylor succeeded to the Presidency of the Church. He had been president of the Twelve.

By birth he was an Englishman, and by adoption first a Canadian and then an American in the narrower sense of the United States. He was born in Milnthorpe, England, on November 1, 1808. Milnthorpe is in Westmorland, a short distance from Windermere, the "queen of English lakes." Both his father and mother were named Taylor, although they do not seem to have been related. Agnes Taylor, John's mother, was descended from the Whitingtons, an illustrious family, one of whom, William Whitington, was knighted by the king, in the fourteenth century.

It was in Penrith, Cumberland, that John spent most of his early life. Penrith is near the Scottish border. Here he learned carpentering, and became interested enough in Methodism to take out a preacher's license. And it was while he was a preacher here that he was strongly impressed with the idea that he had a mission to perform in America. In 1832 he followed his father across the sea and settled in Toronto, Canada. In this part of the New World he continued to preach Methodism, till the year 1836, when he embraced Mormonism. In the meantime he had married.

Before joining his co-religionists in Kirtland, Ohio, the headquarters of the Church, Elder Taylor preached the gospel in Toronto and vicinity. Meanwhile he visited the Saints in Kirtland, and defended the Prophet in the temple. Joseph Smith was then surrounded by apostates, some of whom sought his overthrow as president of the Church. In 1838, after he had changed his residence to Missouri, Elder Taylor was chosen one of the Twelve Apostles. Soon after he was called to go to England on a mission. He was sick at the time, but, nothing daunted, he set out for New York City, where he embarked for Great Britain.

President John Taylor

On returning to America, he took up his residence in Nauvoo. Having considerable literary ability, Elder Taylor was asked by the Prophet to work in the editorial department of the *Times and Seasons,* a Mormon periodical of which Joseph was the editor. Later Elder Taylor established a periodical called *T h e   N a u v o o Neighbor,* a newspaper. At this same time he was a member of the city council. When the Prophet was arrested, in June, 1844, on account of the destruction of the *Expositor,* Elder Taylor was taken with him. And when Joseph and Hyrum were murdered, he was wounded with four bullets.

From 1844 to the time of his elevation to the presidency of the Church Elder Taylor had a varied career.

Once more he was sent on a mission to England, to set in order the churches there in a difficult situation. In 1849 he took a mission to France, where in 1852 he published the *Book of Mormon* in French. Returning home to Utah, he was asked to take a mission to New York City, where he established a periodical called *The Mormon*. Here he defended the Church with great vigor and incisiveness. In the late sixties he and Vice-president Colfax engaged in a spirited debate over the question as to whether or not plural marriage was a matter of religion. Elder Taylor's answer was published in full in the *New York Tribune*. "Who," he demanded, "constituted Mr. Colfax a judge of my religious faith? I think he has stated that 'the faith of every man is a matter between himself and God alone.'" The Colfax articles appeared in the *New York Independent*.

President Taylor's chief characteristics were keen intelligence, exceptional courage, and an intense love of personal liberty. His ruling passion was his desire to be free. His favorite motto was, "The kingdom of God or nothing," and his favorite name, given him in Nauvoo, was "the Champion of Liberty." He sometimes remarked, "I do not believe in a religion that cannot have all my affections, but in a religion for which I can both live and die. I would rather have God for my friend than all other influences and powers."

* * * * *

It was during the administration of President Taylor that the severest attack was made on the doctrine and practice of plural marriage, of which we have spoken very briefly already.

The year 1880 was the fiftieth anniversary of the organization of the Church, of which we shall say more presently. On the occasion of the concluding meeting of the Pioneer Day celebration President Taylor made this prophetic utterance: "There are events in the future, and not far ahead, that will require all our faith, all our energy, all our confidence, all our trust in God, to enable us to withstand the influences that will be brought against us. . . . There never was a time when we needed to be more humble and more prayerful; there never was a time when we needed more fidelity, self-denial, and adherence to the principles of truth than we do this day."

Then came days of sore trial. The Edmunds-Tucker Act was passed and signed. Legal machinery was set in action in Utah. Polygamy was made punishable by fine or imprisonment—usually imprisonment. No man who had more than one wife could act as a juror in any Utah court. In Idaho even those who were members of the Church were disfranchised. No one who believed in polygamy could become a citizen. The Act passed in 1882 was called the Edmunds Act, but in 1887 the Edmunds-Tucker Act gave added powers to the judges who tried polygamy cases. This law required certificates of all marriage to be filed in the offices of the probate courts, it disincorporated the Church of Jesus Christ of Latter-day Saints, ordered the Supreme Court to wind up its affairs, and required that all its property be escheated to the nation. And all this was done in the harshest manner possible, by men who were possessed by the bitterest animosity for the Church.

Thousands of Mormons were disfranchised. A thousand men were imprisoned because they had plural families. Others, hundreds of them, went into exile. Homes were broken up by the cruelties of enforcement. The election machinery was taken out of the hands of the people.

Since the leaders of the Church were particularly sought, President Taylor deemed it advisable to retire from the public eye. It was under these conditions that he died. "President Taylor," said the announcement of his death by his counselors, "has been killed by the cruelty of officals who have in this Territory misrepresented the government of the United States."

* * * * *

But let us turn to a more agreeable subject.

At a general conference of the Church, held in April, 1880, some interesting business was transacted. President Taylor proposed that one-half of the people's indebtedness to the Perpetual Emigration Fund should be remitted. This meant about a million and a half dollars to the Church. (The Perpetual Emigration Fund was established in October, 1849, for the purpose of aiding Saints to emigrate who were too poor to pay for their passage. The money was to be lent them from a revolving fund.) In addition President Taylor agreed to distribute for the Church one thousand cows. The general organization would furnish three hundred and the stakes seven hundred of the thousand; also to distribute five thousand sheep, in the same proportion and manner. This was owing to a drouth that had visited parts of the territory during the previous year (1879.) Moreover, individuals and mercantile institutions were advised to cancel at least part of the amount owed them by poor people. "While God is blessing us," ran the counsel of the leaders, "let us bless one another."

* * * * *

While this persecution of the Latter-day Saints was at its height, with no prospect of diminishing its ardor, President Taylor decided to open up two new fields of refuge for the distressed members of the Church—Mexico and Canada.

Believing that those who had entered upon the practice of plural marriage ought to avoid being prosecuted under the Edmunds-Tucker law, President Taylor sent some men into Mexico, for the purpose of locating a place where these might settle with their families. This was in 1885, while he, with a number of apostles, was making a tour through Arizona. In

1879 Moses Thatcher and James Z. Stewart went to
Mexico, at the request of President Taylor. Three
years later A. W. Ivins, who was in Mexico was asked
to "look for suitable places for colonies in Mexico and
to find out the attitude of the government toward the
establishment of colonies there by the Latter-day
Saints." In 1885 three apostles—Erastus Snow, Brigham Young, Jr., and John W. Taylor—put that question
to President Diaz. The president answered that "the
Mormons would not only be welcome, but the government was anxious for some of them to develop the
country." And he suggested either the state of
Chihuahua or that of Sonora, where, he was sure, they
would be equally welcome. By March, 1885, there was
a settlement of Mormons on the Casas Grandes river,
in Chihuahua. And here they prospered for many
years.

Canada also was settled by some Mormons during
the administration of President Taylor. "In the
latter part of August, 1886," says Charles O. Card
in his narrative, "it was suggested by President Taylor that I explore British Columbia, with a view to
planting a colony of Latter-day Saints north of the
border line. Bishop Isaac E. D. Zundell was selected
to accompany me as Indian interpreter." They paid
most of their own expenses. After exploring the
region around Calgary, in Alberta, Elder Card reported it a suitable place for a colony. And in 1887,
Card, with a company of Saints, returned to the Calgary country. Canada was thus settled from Cache
valley. As soon as they could do so, these first settlers put in crops—potatoes, cabbage, carrots, onions,
and other vegetables. Each man plowed a furrow in
this first Mormon tillage in Canada.

It was during President Taylor's administration,
too, that Mormon settlements were established in
Idaho and Arizona. These were made under the
direction of the apostle Erastus Snow.

Chapter XXIII

THE ADMINISTRATION OF WILFORD WOODRUFF

As already stated, President John Taylor passed away in July, 1887. This left the apostles again in charge of the affairs of the Church. At the head of the quorum was Wilford Woodruff.

This body of priesthood then consisted of the following members: Wilford Woodruff, Lorenzo Snow, Erastus Snow, Franklin D. Richards, Brigham Young, Jr., Moses Thatcher, Francis M. Lyman, John Henry Smith, George Teasdale, Heber J. Grant, and John W. Taylor. There was one vacancy. On the death of President Taylor his two counselors—George Q. Cannon and Joseph F. Smith—took their former places in the quorum. Their positions came immediately after that of Franklin D. Richards and before that of Brigham Young, Jr. After the election by the apostles of President Woodruff to the headship of the Church, Lorenzo Snow became persident of the Quorum of Twelve.

President Woodruff, on his elevation to the presidency, chose George Q. Cannon as his first counselor and Joseph F. Smith as his second counselor. This was in April, 1889, after the apostles had been in charge for twenty-one months. During this time Erastus Snow had passed away. This made three vacancies in the quorum. These were filled by the ordination of Marriner W. Merrill, Anthon H. Lund, and Abraham H. Cannon.

* * * * *

Wilford Woodruff was born in Farmington, now Avon, Connecticut, in March, 1807. His parents were Aphek and Beulah Thompson Woodruff. According to President Woodruff, one of his ancestors was Lord Mayor of London. On both sides his family was long-lived. His trade was that of a miller, at which he worked, mostly for his father, till he was thirty-one.

President Wilford Woodruff

In his *Journal* is a chapter of accidents. He says there: "I have broken both legs, one of them in two places; both arms, both ankles, my breastbone, and three ribs; I have been scalded, frozen, and drowned; I have been in two water wheels while turning under full head; I have passed through a score of hairbreadth escapes. The repeated deliverance from all these remarkable dangers I ascribe to the mercies of my Heavenly Father. In recalling them to mind I always feel impressed to render the gratitude of my heart, with thanksgiving and joy, to the Lord."

Like many others born under similar conditions, President Woodruff had little schooling. "In those days," he explains, "parents did not feel the importance of urging upon their children the advantages of education, as they urge them to-day. They felt that matters of education were wholly confined to the ideas and methods of the school teachers." Nevertheless President Woodruff was an educated man in that he had large contact with men and things and thoughts.

He embraced Mormonism under peculiar circumstances. In 1832 he was impressed to go to Rhode Island, but he went to New York State instead. Had he followed his impression, he likely would have joined the Church then. As it was, he was not baptized till December of the following year. Years before this he had been told by an aged friend named Mason that he would live to become a member of the true Church of Christ—a church with visions and revelations. In 1832 he had read an attack on the Mormons in a newspaper, and had been interested on learning that that organization had apostles and prophets.

On joining the Church young Woodruff wished to become active. He went to Kirtland, Ohio, to see the Prophet. Presently he volunteered to go to Jackson county, Missouri with Zion's camp. When the small army of Mormons was disbanded, Wilford remained in Missouri. There he was overcome with a desire to preach the gospel, but he did not hold the priesthood and did not want to make his desire known. So he went into the forest to pray about the matter. On rising from his knees, he felt that his wish would be granted. Coming out of the woods, he met the presiding officer in the branch of the Church nearby. This man told him he had an impression to send the young man on a mission. Young Woodruff was ordained a priest, after which he went on his first mission.

* * * * *

In April, 1839, he was called to the apostleship by the Prophet. The following spring he went to England, with most of his fellow apostles. And there he had some most extraordinary experiences.

On the evening of his thirty-third birthday, March 1, 1840, he was preaching in the town of Hanley. Here is what he says about it in his *Journal*:

While we were singing the first hymn, the Spirit of the Lord rested upon me, and the voice of God said unto me: "This is the last meeting that you will hold with this people for many days." I was astonished at this, as I had many appointments out in the district. When I arose to speak to the people, I told them that it was the last meeting I should hold with them for many days. They were as much astonished as I was. At the close of the meeting four persons came forward for baptism; we went down into the water and baptized them.

In the morning I went in secret before the Lord, and asked him what was his will concerning me. The answer I received was that I should go to the south; for the Lord had a great work for me to perform there, as many souls were waiting for his word.

In fulfillment of the directions given me, I took coach and rode to Wolverhampton, twenty-six miles, spending the night there. On the morning of the 4th I again took coach and rode through Dudley, Stourbridge, Stourport, and Worcester, then walked a number of miles to Mr. John Benbow's Hill Farm, Castle Frome, Ledbury, Herefordshire. This was a farming country in the south of England.

I found Mr. Benbow to be a wealthy farmer, cultivating three hundred acres of land, occupying a good mansion, and having plenty of means. His wife Jane had no children. I presented myself to him as a missionary from America, an elder of the Church of Jesus Christ of Latter-day Saints, who had been sent to him by commandment of God as a messenger of salvation, to preach the gospel of life to him and his household and the inhabitants of the land. He and his wife received me with glad hearts and thanksgiving. It was in the evening when I arrived. After receiving refreshments we sat down together and conversed until two o'clock in the morning.

I rejoiced greatly when Mr. Benbow told me that there was a company of men and women—over six hundred in number—who had broken off from the Wesleyan Methodists, and taken the name of United Brethren. They had forty-five preachers among them, and had chapels and many houses that were licensed according to the law. This body of United Brethren were searching for light and truth, but had gone as far as they could, and were calling upon the Lord continually to open the way before them and send them light and knowledge, that they might know the true way to be saved.

Mr. Benbow had in his mansion a large hall which was licensed for preaching. He sent word through the neighborhood that an American missionary would preach at his house that evening. Many neighbors came in, and I preached. I also preached at the same place on the following evening. Six persons were baptized, including Mr. Benbow, his wife, and four preachers of the United Brethren. I spent most of the following day in clearing out the pool of water and preparing it for baptizing. I afterwards baptized six hundred persons in that pool. . . .

The first thirty days after my arrival in Herefordshire, I had baptized forty-five preachers and one hundred and sixty members of the United Brethren, who put into my hands one chapel and forty-five houses, which were licensed. This opened a wide field for labor, and enabled me to bring into the Church, through the blessings of God, over eighteen hundred souls during the eight months, including all of the six hundred United Brethren, except one person. In this number were also some two hundred preachers of various denominations.

Other activities of Elder Woodruff may be mentioned here, but not treated with the fulness they deserve. He was one of the outstanding pioneers in Utah. For twenty-five years he was president of the Agricultural and Industrial Association in the territory. Also he traveled extensively among the Saints in the United States.

* * * * *

One of the things for which President Woodruff will always be remembered by a grateful people is his habit of writing whatever happened that he looked upon as important. It is to this habit that we owe many sayings and teachings of the Prophet Joseph Smith. He did this in response to the advice of President Smith to the Twelve Apostles.

President Woodruff lived a simple life. Naturally a tireless worker, he was always busy either at physical labor or in the ministry. Idleness was foreign to his nature. It is said that in physical toil he could do the work of two ordinary men.

Perhaps his main trait was a great susceptibility to the promptings of the Holy Spirit. We have alluded to this on more than one occasion. A particular example was his missionary labors in Herefordshire. "The whole history of this mission," he says in his *Journal*, "shows the importance of listening to the still, small voice of the Spirit of God and the revelations of the Holy Ghost." In the year 1855 he set this in his *Diary*: "After retiring to bed I prayed to the Lord to show me what we should teach the people, and this I received as an answer: 'Let my servants obtain the Holy Ghost and keep my Spirit with them, and that will instruct them what to teach people continually. Instruct the people to keep my Spirit with them, and they will be enabled to understand the word of the Lord when it is taught to them.' "

Being in constant possession of the Holy Spirit and listening to its dictates—that may be said to have been the motto of Wilford Woodruff.

* * * * *

His administration as president of the Church extended from April, 1889, to September, 1898—a period of nine years and five months.

For the first three years of this time, as well as during the time the apostles were in charge of Church affairs following the death of President Taylor, the anti-polygamy crusade was on. But either it was conducted on a less cruel basis or the Mormon people had adjusted themselves to the new conditions. At any rate, their sufferings were not quite so great. The times were troublous enough, however, for the Saints to feel the pressure. Meantime the Supreme Court of the United States was considering the question of the constitutionality of the Edmunds-Tucker law. And when the law was declared constitutional by the highest court in the land, the Mormons gave up the struggle to maintain the practice of the principle of plural marriage. They had contended all along that plural marriage, both in principle and practice, was a part of their religion, and that the Congress had no right Joseph Smith, which anticipated just such a situation.

or to prohibit the exercise of any religious practice. The Supreme Court decided otherwise, and so President Woodruff, in 1890, issued a declaration, in which he advised the Saints against entering upon the practice of plural marriage. Here is the essential part of the text of the Manifesto:

> Inasmuch as laws have been enacted by Congress forbidding plural marriages, which laws have been pronounced constitutional by the court of last resort, I hereby declare my intention to submit to those laws, and to use my influence with the members of the Church over which I preside to have them do likewise. . . . I now publicly declare that my advice to the Latter-day Saints is to refrain from contracting any marriage forbidden by the law of the land.

This Manifesto was submitted to the general conference of the Church, held in Salt Lake City, Utah, October 6, 1890, and, on motion of President Lorenzo Snow, then at the head of the quorum of Twelve Apostles, it was unaminously sustained. Since then no polygamous marriage has been performed in the United States by authority of the Church.

In view of the fact that the principle of plural marriage was revealed by revelation to the Prophet and further that the practice of this principle in the Church was commanded by the Lord the question may be asked, and often has been asked: How can the Mormons reconcile their action to obey a political law rather than a law of God?

The answer is to be found in a revelation to Joseph Smith, which anticipated just such a situation. It was given in January, 1841. "Verily, verily," says a passage in this revelation, "I say unto you, that when I give a commandment to any of the sons of men to do a work unto my name, and those sons of men go with all their might and with all they have to perform that work, and cease not their diligence, and their enemies come upon them and hinder them from performing that work, behold, it behooveth me to require that work no more at the hands of those sons of men, but to

accept their offerings. And the iniquity and transgression of my holy laws and commandments I will
visit upon the heads of those who hindered my work,
unto the third and fourth generation, so long as they
repent not, and hate me, saith the Lord God." A
specific application of this idea was made in the revelation to the establishment of a city and a temple in
Jackson county, Missouri, but it was applied equally
to the situation in which the Latter-day Saints were
forced to give up the practice of plural marriage.

The results of this declaration were almost immediate. First of all, the old political alignment in
Utah—the People's Party, composed of Mormons and
their sympathizers, and the Liberal Party, made up of
the opponents of the Mormons—was broken up and
the national parties of Democrats and Republicans
were organized. Secondly, there grew up a tacit understanding that those who had entered into the plural
marriage system before the Manifesto should not be
prosecuted. Third, the President of the United States
—Benjamin Harrison—on a petition of the First
Presidency of the Church, issued a proclamation of
amnesty, in December, 1891, to polygamists for
offences committed prior to November 1, 1890. Fourth,
in the year 1896, during the administration of Grover
Cleveland, Utah was admitted to the Union as a state.

* * * * *

Two other events in the administration of President Woodruff deserve mention. One was the tour
to the East made by the Tabernacle Choir; the other,
the religious bigotry that kept the Saints from being
represented in the World's Parliament of Religions.

From the very beginning the Latter-day Saints
have encouraged music in their congregations. As
early as July, 1830, Emma Smith, wife of the Prophet,
was required to make "a selection of sacred hymns"
for the Church. And in this connection the Lord
said, "My soul delighteth in the song of the heart; yea,
the song of the righteous is a prayer unto me, and it
shall be answered with a blessing upon their heads."

In accordance with this request a collection of hymns was made in America; and, in 1840, another collection for the use of the Saints in Great Britain.

In the Utah period composers arose to put to music words that had been written by such early poets as Parley P. Pratt and William W. Phelps. Outstanding among these composers were George Careless and Evan Stephens, converts to the Faith. A new group of poets, too, arose—notably Eliza R. Snow-Smith, in the early period, and Orson F. Whitney, in the later period of Utah history. The present *Psalmody* is made up mostly of words and music by Mormon writers and composers. In the Utah period of the Church, also, the Tabernacle Choir, with from two to five hundred voices, has been an inspiration to millions, especially when accompanied by the famous Tabernacle organ.

In 1893 the Choir, with President Woodruff and other officials of the Church, went to Chicago. The World's Fair was then the main attraction there. Many choirs competed. The Tabernacle Choir took second prize. It gave several concerts on the way there and the return, which drew high praise from music critics.

At the time the Exposition was held in Chicago there was a Parliament of Religions. This began in September, 1893. To this gathering all the religions of the world, pagan as well as Christian, were invited—except the Church of Jesus Christ of Latter-day Saints. The First Presidency of the Church, however, asked to be represented, and appointed President Brigham H. Roberts, a member of the First Council of Seventy, to prepare an address for the occasion, in the event their request for a hearing should be granted. He was not permitted to present his case, however, before the large assembly of Christians, Jews, and pagans, but was allowed the privilege of reading his paper in one of the committee rooms, which would seat about fifty persons. He declined to do that. And in the newspapers he exposed the narrow-mindedness of the Parliament officials—much to their embarrassment.

Chapter XXIV

LATTER-DAY SAINT TEMPLES

Joseph Smith, like many others before him, asked himself: What is to become of those good people who lived before Christ? What is the fate of those who, after his time, did not have the opportunity of hearing the gospel? And he answered these questions, through revelation, in temple work. The gospel is broad enough to cover all the children of men—those who have lived and those who will yet live, as well as those who are alive now. "It is no more incredible," said the Prophet in 1841, "that God should *save* the dead than that he should *raise* the dead." And that is what the gospel proposes to do—give the opportunity of salvation to all mankind, whether they are dead or alive.

In Mormon theology men do not really "die." What they do when they "die" is to pass from one sphere of existence to another; only, in the passing they sluff the physical body as they would a cloak. It is the spirit, after all, that thinks, and feels, and acts, and wills, not the tabernacle of flesh. And the human spirit, as the Church teaches, lived before it took on a mortal body, and it will continue to live after it leaves the house of clay. At "death," which is only a separation of the spirit and the body of flesh, the body returns to earth, whence it came, and the spirit enters the spirit world, to await the resurrection. In the resurrection the two are reunited under conditions of immortality. Thus, while the body undergoes changes, the spirit remains essentially the same. It thinks, wills and acts without interruption. It is the enduring thing about us.

Now, according to the religion of Jesus Christ as understood by the Latter-day Saints, the gospel is preached to the "dead." If the gospel is necessary at all, it is as necessary for the "dead" as for the "living."

"Salvation," however, in the Mormon view, is different from "exaltation." Just as all mankind will die on account of Adam's transgression, so all mankind will be raised from the dead through the blood of Christ; and that without anything on their part. But to be "exalted" they must believe, repent of their sins, be baptized for the remission of their sins, be confirmed by the imposition of hands, and thereafter endeavor sincerely to live a life in accordance with gospel standards.

This doctrine of "salvation for the dead" clears up many things that have been obscure in the religion of Jesus Christ. First, it puts all men on the same plane. Second, it represents God as a God of justice, mercy, and universal love. Third, it opens the way for a true conception of the universality of the gospel. Thus Mormonism becomes a faith that is universal in a sense not heretofore perceived by the average Christian.

* * * * *

It is necessary for some reason that the ordinances for the dead shall be performed in houses specially built for the purpose. This is made clear by the Prophet Joseph Smith. In a revelation to him occurs this passage: "This ordinance (baptism for the dead) belongeth to my house, and cannot be acceptable to me, only in the days of your poverty, wherein ye are not able to build a house unto me. But I command you, all ye my saints, to build a house unto me."

The revelation in which this passage occurs was given in January, 1841, just as the Saints were beginning to settle Nauvoo and when they were almost destitute of property. The principle of "salvation for the dead" had not been known by even the Prophet very long before this. As soon, therefore, as the idea was seen in all its clearness, steps were taken to "do work for the dead." The first baptisms were performed in

the Mississippi river, but only because there was no
house in which the ordinance could be performed.

The Latter-day Saints have other sacred ordinances that are dependent in the same way on sacred
places—houses of the Lord. There are, for instance,
the ordinance of marriage for eternity as well as for
time, and sealings of parents and children and husbands
and wives, for both the living and the dead. All these
are as necessary for those who have lived as for those
who are now living. This is the use to which, in the
main, the temples are put by the Latter-day Saints.

*   *   *   *   *

Thus far nine temples have been erected in this
dispensation—at Kirtland, Ohio, at Nauvoo, Illinois,
at St. George, Utah, at Logan, Utah, at Manti, Utah,
at Salt Lake City, Utah, at Cardston, Canada, at Laie,
Hawaii, and at Mesa, Arizona. Two others are in con-
templation; one will be in Idaho Falls, Idaho and the
other in Los Angeles, California.

The Kirtland Temple was begun in 1833, as soon
as Zion's Camp was disbanded and the Prophet returned to Kirtland; and it was dedicated in March,
1836. It cost about seventy-five thousand dollars.
At the time of the dedication many visions and revelations were given to the Prophet and others. Here
Christ appeared to Joseph Smith and Oliver Cowdery;
also Moses, Elijah, and Elias. Moses gave them the
"keys" of the gathering of Israel; Elijah the "keys" of
salvation for the dead. No ordinances for the dead,
however, were performed in the Kirtland Temple.

The Nauvoo Temple was a more prententious
structure. It was planned to cost one million dollars.
The corner stone was laid in April, 1841; it was dedicated after the Prophet's death in 1846, while most
of the Saints were on their way to the West. Like the
Kirtland Temple, this temple was dedicated before it
was entirely finished—as to some of the inside rooms.
But all the ordinances for the living and the dead were
performed in the Nauvoo Temple. Prior to the death

TEMPLES OF THE CHURCH OF JESUS CHRIST OF LATTER-DAY SAINTS
Cardston, Alberta, Canada   Mesa, Arizona
Laie, Hawaiian Islands   Salt Lake City, Utah   Manti, Utah
Logan, Utah   St. George, Utah

of the Prophet baptisms for the dead were performed there.

The St. George Temple was the first one to be dedicated in Utah. It was begun and finished during the administration of President Brigham Young. In April, 1877, four months before President Young's death, the general conference of the Church was held in St. George. The temple was dedicated at that time. The dedicatory prayer was offered by President Daniel H. Wells.

The Logan Temple, begun in the closing year of President Young's administration, was dedicated by President John Taylor, in May, 1884. Situated on an eminence to the east of the town, it commands a view of the beautiful and fertile Cache valley. The dedicatory services were impressive to a degree that proved satisfying to those who participated in them. As the St. George Temple serves the Saints in the extreme southern part of Utah, so the Logan Temple serves all who live in northern Utah and southeastern Idaho.

The Manti Temple is in Sanpete county, about midway between the St. George Temple and the Logan Temple. It was begun in 1877, during the presidency of Brigham Young, who had selected the site in 1875, but it was not finished till 1888, after President Taylor's death. The dedicatory prayer was offered by President Lorenzo Snow. Like the Logan Temple, this structure stands on a hill northeast of the town—the most conspicuous and imposing object in the valley.

The Salt Lake Temple was the first building of its kind to be planned in the West by the Saints. That was when the pioneer company was still in the valley of the Salt Lake. It is the most stately and beautiful of the Mormon temples, also. Forty years it took to complete this building—from the time the corner stones were laid till its dedication, in April 1893. After the capstone was laid the previous year, work was speeded up. Forty thousand people witnessed the laying of the capstone—the largest gathering in the history of the

Church up to that time. The dedicatory services continued till more than eighty-five thousand members of the Church had attended them. The dedicatory prayer was offered by President Woodruff. It was a memorable day when these services were begun.

The Cardston Temple, in Canada, was the first temple to be erected outside the United States. The site was chosen by President Joseph F. Smith, in 1913, a few years before his death. The corner stones were laid under the direction of President David O. McKay. "The building is a square, measuring 165 feet each way, 110 feet high, and is lifted up by an artistic retaining wall enclosing a space of 235 feet each way, each side facing the four main points of the compass. The entrance is on the west through the annex. The structure is built of granite from the famous Katoonai Lake district, British Columbia." This temple was dedicated in 1923 by President Heber J. Grant.

The Hawaiian Temple is the first building of its kind to be erected outside the Americas. The site was chosen, in 1915, by the late President Joseph F. Smith, and dedicated then. This was on the birthday of President Brigham Young, who had prophesied that some day there would be a temple with gardens on its roof. The prophecy was fulfilled in the erection of the Hawaiian Temple. The building measures 102 by 78 feet, and is one story in height. The dedicatory prayer was offered by President Heber J. Grant, in November, 1919.

The Arizona Temple site was chosen by President Heber J. Grant, in November, 1921, at the time when the Maricopa stake conference was held. The site covers forty acres of ground. The building rests on a foundation base 180 feet by 195 feet, and is 66 feet high. It was dedicated in October, 1927, by President Grant.

Chapter XXV

THE ADMINISTRATION OF LORENZO SNOW

As already stated President Woodruff passed away in September, 1898, at the age of ninety-one. This left the Twelve Apostles once more in charge of the affairs of the Church. They were in charge, however, only from September 2, when President Woodruff died, to September 13, when his successor was chosen. President Lorenzo Snow was at the head of the Church from that date to October 10, 1901, when he passed away at the age of eighty-seven, a period of a little more than three years.

This was the shortest time that any president had presided over the Church. Joseph Smith had been president fourteen years, Brigham Young thirty-one years, John Taylor seven years, and Wilford Woodruff nine years. These men, when they came into the presidency, were twenty-seven, forty-six, seventy-two, and eighty-two, respectively. President Snow was eighty-four years old when he became president.

* * * * *

Lorenzo Snow was born in Mantua, Ohio, April 3, 1814, the fifth child and the first son in the family of Oliver Snow. The Snows were sociable people and their home was a gathering place for the intellectual in that part of Ohio. One of the constant visitors to the home was Sidney Rigdon, who was then a leader in the Campbellite Church. In his home, too, as we ought to remember, was Lorenzo's sister, Eliza, who even then was writing poetry for the periodicals and who was to become widely known as the author of the hymn, "O My Father."

From the time he could read Lorenzo was a student, and generally was found, as his companions used to say, "hid up with his book." This habit of reading stayed with him through life. "With the exception of one term in the high school at Ravenna," says his famous sister, "and a special term of tuition under a Hebrew professor, he completed his scholastic training in Oberlin College, which at that time was exclusively a Presbyterian institution.

President Lorenzo Snow

Through the solicitation of an intimate friend, conected with the college, he was induced to enter, and through this friend's influence, as a special favor, he was admitted."

Despite the fact that in his home there was a strong religious atmosphere Lorenzo showed no inclination for the religious life. He did not join any church. When he went to Oberlin, this disinclination for the church increased. And he wrote to his sister: "If there is nothing better than is to be found here in Oberlin College, goodbye to all religion." Yet he was intimately associated with both the students and the teachers there.

By this time his sister, Eliza, had embraced Mormonism and gone to Kirtland, where she lived in the Prophet's home and tutored his and other children.

Her letters about the new church aroused Lorenzo's interest. And when Professor Seixas was asked to go to Kirtland to teach Hebrew, Lorenzo followed him. Professor Seixas was one of the instructors in Oberlin College. One day, not long after his arrival in Kirtland, the young man was informed by Patriarch Joseph Smith: "You will soon be convinced of the latter-day work and be baptized." And this was so. For in June, 1836, he was baptized by Elder John T. Boynton, one of the Twelve Apostles. Some time later, as he was taking his usual walk, he received a positive knowledge that the new movement was of God, and in this testimony he never wavered during the sixty-five years of his membership in the Church.

* * * * *

It was the custom in the early days of the Church for the men, as soon as they were baptized, to go out and preach the gospel to those who had not yet heard it. Lorenzo Snow did this. Not long after his baptism he took a mission in Ohio, partly among his relatives. He traveled without money. That was the custom in those times. The first day he "walked upwards of twenty miles." His first "gospel conversation" was with his father's sister, a Mrs. Granger. And he held a number of meetings in her home. The next day he traveled thirty miles. Time after time he was refused a meal or a night's lodging at the end of his journey. At last a man took him in, but he went supperless to bed. By this time he was near an uncle's home, in Medina county, Ohio. Here he held his first public meeting. "It was a sore trial," he says of this mission, "to face that audience in the capacity of a preacher." But he gave them a good sermon, for he had fasted and prayed to that end. A second meeting was held in the court house. One of that congregation became his wife. And on one occasion a trap was laid for him—which he escaped by a stroke of inspiration.

Such was this young convert's first experience preaching the gospel.

In the spring of 1840 he was called on a mission to England. As the reader may remember, eight of the apostles were there already. He borrowed money for his passage, at heavy interest, he tells us. He was not yet married. On his return to Nauvoo, he electioneered for Joseph Smith, who was a candidate for the presidency of the United States. Elder Snow informs us that many persons whom he met looked with favor on the candidacy of the Mormon leader, and would have voted for him if the Prophet had lived. Elder Snow had intended not to marry, but to devote all his time to the ministry. However, after his leader told him the importance of marriage in the scheme of the gospel, he married.

* * * * *

Lorenzo Snow did a notable work in Brigham City in the early days of Utah. By this time he was an apostle, one of the Twelve; he had been ordained in 1849, with three others. Also he had had a remarkable experience in introducing the gospel to the Italians, particularly in the Piedmont valley, Italy. So he was well qualified by experience, as well as by knowledge, to establish a community life in accordance with the principles of revealed religion. President Young called him to go to Brigham City, to lead the colony there.

Beginning in the simplest way, as we have seen, he organized the community socially, economically, and religiously. He became a captain of industry.

And then, in 1898, on the death of President Woodruff, he was called to the presidency of the Church. This was exactly eleven days afterwards.

The new presiding officer was entering upon his eighty-fifth year. He had been in the Church for sixty-two years, and an apostle for forty-nine years. As his counselors he selected the two men who had served in this capacity with President Taylor and President Woodruff—George Q. Cannon and Joseph F.

Smith. Notwithstanding his extreme age, President Snow was hale in body and clear in mind.

When the new president took office the quorum of Twelve was left with the following membership: Franklin D. Richards and Brigham Young, Jr., who had been appointed by President Young; Francis M. Lyman, John Henry Smith, George Teasdale, Heber J. Grant, and John W. Taylor, all of whom had received their appointment from President Taylor; Marriner W. Merrill, Anthon H. Lund, Mathias F. Cowley, and Abraham O. Woodruff, all of whom had been appointed in the previous administration. To fill the vacancy created by his appointment, President Snow called Rudger Clawson to the apostleship, and later, when Franklin D. Richards passed away, he appointed Reed Smoot to the vacancy.

* * * * *

Three events stand out in the administration of President Snow. These are the exclusion of Brigham H. Roberts from the national House of Representatives, the opening of a mission to Japan, and the effort to increase the tithing of the Church members to the point where the financial burden of the organization might begin to be lifted from the shoulders of the people.

The exclusion of Brigham H. Roberts from the House was a religious matter (1) because he had embraced a tenet of the Church against which a great deal of opposition had been created by church people in every part of the Union, and (2) because his exclusion had really been brought about by the religious agitators of the country, as was then supposed.

Mr. Roberts had been duly elected Representative to the Congress on the Democratic ticket. This was in November, 1898. It was generally known in Utah that he was a polygamist—he had two wives, both of whom he had married before the Manifesto. In addition, he was one of the seven presidents of the Seventy—a general officer in the Church. Since, however, it was understood that those men who had entered upon the polygamous marriage practice before 1890 would not be prosecuted but allowed to retain their families as they had been doing, no one thought that the Congress would have any objections. And so, after the election, Mr. Roberts made preparations to assume his office at the national capital.

But meantime the forces of opposition in Utah, led by a ministerial association there, interested themselves. Was the old question to be revived? It seemed so. One of their contentions was that the Mormon Church had broken its pledge to the Federal government, and was again taking up with plural marriage and practicing it. President Snow issued a denial, and this denial was published in the *New York World*. The simple fact is that, as pointed out by Senator Joseph L. Rawlins in the Senate at the time, there was no understanding between the Mormons and the Federal government that "polygamists should be disqualified to vote or to hold office."

Nevertheless Congressman-elect Roberts was excluded from his seat in the lower house. The reason was clear. Petitions from every part of the nation deluged Congressmen, and so, when the question of seating the man from Utah came up, they voted by an overwhelming majority not to allow him to sit. They were probably afraid to risk their re-election by voting against the resolution to seat him. Many of the Congressmen said so afterwards. In those days prejudice against the Latter-day Saints was very strong.

* * * * *

Considerable interest was shown in the opening of the mission to Japan.

In February, 1901, the apostle Heber J. Grant was chosen to introduce the gospel to the Japanese nation. With him went Elders Horace Ensign, Louis A. Kelsch, and Alma O. Taylor. They arrived in Yokohama, Japan, in August of that year, and began work immediately.

Progress, however, was very slow, for more than one reason. In the first place, the missionaries had to learn the Japanese language, and that was made all the more difficult because, whenever they attempted to converse with the Japanese, the latter would switch to English, because they wanted to learn English. And then, too, the habits of life and thought of the Japanese, as well as their religion, were unlike those of the peoples among whom they had lived. It is little wonder, then, that there was not much in the way of results from the labors of the missionaries. However, a translation of the *Book of Mormon* was made, and published in 1909.

When the elders returned—that is, Elders Grant, Ensign, and Kelsch—they left Elder Taylor in charge of the mission. Later other missionaries joined Elder Taylor, but the results obtained did not justify any further work among the Japanese. Hence they were all withdrawn. Now there are no missionaries in Japan, although some converts remain to testify to the establishment of a mission among that people, and there is a special mission in the Hawaiian Islands among the Japanese residents there.

* * * * *

Perhaps the outstanding event in the administration of President Snow is the revival of the payment of tithing by the members of the Church.

Money with which to operate the Church is obtained through a tithing system under which each member is supposed to pay one-tenth of his interest annually to the Church, for its maintenance.

Certain things, however, had contributed to lessen the tithing receipts and to bring about indebtedness.

For one thing, during the administrations of Presidents Taylor and Woodruff intense opposition, not to say persecution, had greatly disturbed the finances of the Church. It was a time, as the reader may recall, when the anti-polygamy laws were being enacted and enforced. And in those days, as the reader already knows, most of the authorities of the organization were "underground"—that is, in hiding from the Federal officials.

And then, for another thing, when the property of the Mormon Church was confiscated by the Federal government, the members of the Church thought: What is the use of contributing to an organization when what we pay in for one purpose is taken by outsiders and used for another purpose? There was a time when the Church had to pay rent to the Federal government for the use of the Tabernacle in Salt Lake City! Thus the amount of tithing dwindled, and the debts of the Church increased. Hence, when there was a new situation to meet in the time of President Snow; something had to be done to bring relief from a condition into which the Church had inevitably fallen.

The remedy was natural. The Lord had established the principle of tithing as the way in which the Church was to raise money. The thing to do, therefore was to preach tithing to the people. So President Snow, beginning in St. George, as President Young had so often done before him, proclaimed a renewal of the law of tithing. This was in the spring of 1899. A tremendous impetus was given to the idea at a conference of the Mutual Improvement Associations, held in Salt Lake City, in May of this year, by the adoption of the following statement: "Resolved: That we accept the doctrine of tithing, as now presented by President Snow, as the present word of the Lord unto us, and we do accept it with all our hearts; we will ourselves observe it, and we will do all in our power to get the Latter-day Saints to do likewise." In addition, a solemn fast day was proclaimed for this conference and for all the Saints, on Sunday, July 2, 1899.

The effect of all this agitation for tithing was that money poured into the Church from this source. Bonds to the amount of one million dollars, which had been issued to concentrate the indebtedness of of the Church, were presently taken up; and, in the administration of Joseph F. Smith, the Church was declared to be free of debt. And it has remained so from that day to this.

Chapter XXVI

THE ADMINISTRATION OF JOSEPH F. SMITH

Once more, at the death of President Lorenzo Snow, the quorum of Twelve Apostles took the direction of the affairs of the Church. Not for long, however, for the First Presidency was reorganized seven days after the passing of President Snow. The apparent haste in this action lay in the fact that the financial interests of the Church required the designation of the Trustee in Trust—an office which, since the time of Joseph Smith, has been held by the President of the Church. Besides, there was no point to be gained by waiting.

The new president was Joseph F. Smith. President Smith had been a member of the Council of the Twelve since October, 1867, when he was then but twenty-nine years of age. And then, too, he had been a counselor in the First Presidency since 1880—twenty-one years. In fact, as we have seen, he had been counselor to three presidents—John Taylor, Wilford Woodruff, and Lorenzo Snow. As his counselors he chose John R. Winder, who up to that time had been in the Presiding Bishopric, and Anthon H. Lund, one of the apostles appointed by President Woodruff.

After the elevation of Joseph F. Smith to the Presidency and that of Anthon H. Lund to the First Presidency, the quorum membership stood: Brigham Young, Jr., Francis M. Lyman, John Henry Smith, George Teasdale, Heber J. Grant, John W. Taylor, Marriner W. Merrill, Mathias F. Cowley, Abraham O. Woodruff, Rudger Clawson, Reed Smoot. The promotion of Anthon H. Lund to the First Presidency created a vacancy in the quorum of Twelve, and this was filled by the appointment of

Hyrum M. Smith, a son of President Smith.

During the presidency of Joseph F. Smith, which continued from October 17, 1901, to November 19, 1918, a little more than seventeen years, eleven apostles were appointed. Their names are: Hyrum M. Smith, George Albert Smith, Charles W. Penrose, George F. Richards, Orson F. Whitney, David O. McKay, Anthony W. Ivins, Joseph Fielding Smith, James E. Talmage, Stephen L Richards and Richard R. Lyman. This was due partly to deaths and partly to the taking of apostles into the First Presidency. In March, 1910, President Winder passed away. President Lund was thereupon made first counselor and the apostle John Henry Smith, chosen second counselor. In October, 1911, Counselor Smith died, and Charles W. Penrose took his place in the First Presidency. And then, too, three of the apostles passed away, and two resigned.

President Joseph F. Smith

*   *   *   *   *

President Joseph F. Smith was born in Far

West, Missouri, November 13, 1838.   He was the
son of Hyrum Smith, brother of the Prophet Joseph.
At the time of his birth his father was in prison,
with the Prophet and several other Mormon leaders,
and the whole Mormon people in Missouri were on
the point of being expelled from the state.   Joseph
F. Smith's mother was Mary Fielding, who was converted by Parley P. Pratt in Canada.

The first eight years of his life Joseph F. spent
in Nauvoo.   He was in his sixth year when the Prophet and his father were killed in Carthage, Illinois.
With his mother and her brother, Joseph Fielding, the
boy Joseph, now in his ninth year, crossed the plains
in a covered wagon.   Most of the way he drove a team
of oxen.   On reaching Salt Lake valley, the family
made a home in the southeastern part of the town.
In September, 1852, the mother passed away.   Joseph
was then fourteen years old.

At fifteen Joseph F. began his public activity.
He was called on a mission to Hawaii, then the Sandwich Islands, to preach the gospel to the natives.
With eighteen other elders he left home in May,
1854.   Arriving in the San Bernardino valley, the
missionaries found themselves without funds.   It will
be remembered that this valley had been settled
since the year 1851 by the apostles Amasa M. Lyman
and Charles C. Rich, with a company of Saints from
the Salt Lake valley.   So Joseph and some of the
other missionaries went to work making shingles.
Later some Australian converts came along and
bought their horses—which gave them the necessary
money for their passage to Honolulu.

Elder Smith, on his arrival in his field of labor,
was assigned to the island of Maui.   This was the
scene of the labors of Elder George Q. Cannon,
not long before this.   For two months Elder Smith
worked with the language, to master it sufficiently
to preach to the natives.   At the end of this time
he was assured by his companion, that he could

speak it well enough to begin missionary work. In a hundred days from his arrival on the island, part of which time he had been ill, he had mastered the language to the point where he could preach and converse freely and accurately. Ten years afterwards Elder Smith went on another mission to the islands, with the apostle Ezra T. Benson to set in order the affairs of the Church there. All through his life Elder Smith, whenever he met any natives of the islands, spoke to them in their own tongue.

On returning home from that first mission, which he did in 1857 when Johnston's army was on its way to the Salt Lake valley, he married, was ordained a high priest, and became a member of the high council in the Salt Lake stake. But in 1860 he was called on another mission, this time to Great Britain. The apostles Lyman, Rich, and Cannon were then presiding over the mission. He was released to return home in 1863. On reaching New York, however, Elder Smith found that his funds had run out. He was compelled to remain in the metropolis till another company of emigrants came along, in which he could cross the plains. Meantime he worked for the necessary means.

* * * * *

Three years after he returned from his European mission, he was made an apostle. This was in July, 1866. From now on, therefore, his public activities were greatly increased. At the same time he was set apart as one of President Young's counselors—not a regular, but a special counselor. For Brigham Young, like Joseph Smith, at one time had seven counselors. In 1874 he took another mission to England, but he did not stay there more than a year. On his return home he was appointed president of the Davis stake. In 1877 he was sent again to England, but returned home when President Young died. Meantime, for a little while, Elder Smith made his home in Provo, and became a councilman in the town government. Also he was a member of the city council in Salt Lake City and a member of the legislature of the Territory of Utah. He served in the legislature for seven consecutive terms. This was in the lower house. For two terms he was a Territorial senator. Over one of the conventions called to draft a constitution for a proposed state government, he was elected president. The passage of the anti-polygamy laws disqualified him from holding further political positions.

Away back in 1869 Wilford Woodruff and Joseph F. Smith were attending a quarterly conference of the Church in the Juab stake. On Sunday morning "they attended a Sunday School session, which was held in the old Social Hall. Elder Woodruff . . . turned to Elder Joseph F. Smith and asked him to arise to his feet. Elder Smith complied. 'Look at him, children,' Wilford Woodruff said, 'for he resembles the Prophet Joseph more than any living man. He will become President of the Church of Jesus Christ of Latter-day Saints.'" Seven days after the death of President Snow, as we have seen— that is, thirty-two years after the prophecy was uttered—Joseph F. Smith was made President of the Church.

President Smith's nature was intense. His devotion to the cause of Mormonism was deep, complete, and unquestioned. By nature he was exceptionally clear in his ideas, and very positive. What he believed, he believed with his whole heart; what he knew, he knew with every fiber of his being. And his expression of truth was such that no one could misunderstand. He was deeply spiritual. Intuitively he went to the heart of any problem with which he had to deal. He was outstanding in his insight into spiritual truth. Moreover, he was unusually versatile. Always he had something new to say, or a new way of saying it. No one who ever heard him speak in the pulpit had any doubt as to his sincerity or his knowledge of the gospel.

His administration, as many readers of this will know from their own experience, fell in a critical period of the world. A president of the United States was murdered—William McKinley, and the World War broke out in Europe, and involved the United States of America. At the time of President Smith's death in November, 1918 the devastating influenza swept the country, and his funeral services had to be held out-of-doors, in the cemetery.

*   *   *   *   *

Several important events stand out in the administration of President Smith.

Perhaps the most disturbing of these was what is known as the Smoot case. In January, 1903, the legislature of Utah elected Reed Smoot to the United States Senate. This was after Utah had been admitted to statehood and before the amendment to the Federal Constitution providing for the election of senators by the people. The fact that Reed Smoot was also an apostle was made a pretext for a protest against his being seated at the Capital. While he was not a polygamist, yet he *believed* in the principle of plural marriage as the Latter-day Saints had practiced it while the law' permitted. And that was enough, the protestants thought, to keep him from being seated. It will be recalled that Brigham H. Roberts had been excluded from the House of Representatives because he was a polygamist. Now, however, it was proposed to punish a man for his beliefs. The protest originated in Salt Lake City. Nineteen citizens signed the petition. Of these nineteen persons four were ministers; indeed the first signature on the petition was that of a minister, a bitter anti-Mormon. Others were politicians.

Three of the six points in this protest had to do with polygamy. It was charged that the leaders of the Church, of whom Reed Smoot was one, "connived at and encouraged the practice of polygamy

and polygamous cohabitation" and "protected and
honored the violators of the laws against polygamy
and polygamous cohabitation." The other points
dilated upon the dominance of the priesthood and
the concentration of this priesthood in the general
authorities of the Church, including Reed Smoot. One
of these protestants, a preacher, made a separate affidavit, in which he declared that Mr. Smoot was
a polygamist—a statement generally known to be
untrue.

In March, 1904, however, Mr. Smoot was sworn
in as a senator and given his seat in the Upper House.
This gave him an advantage. It was necessary,
then, to unseat him. The committee appointed to
hear the evidence sat from January 1904, to June,
1906. As the hearing progressed, Reed Smoot was
all but lost sight of, and the Church of Jesus Christ
of Latter-day Saints became more and more prominent in the committee room. President Smith and
other leaders of the organization were called upon
to testify in the case. And in general they were
treated with great discourtesy by members of the
committee. Some of them were openly insulted,
others were derided for their religious views. And
all this, one must bear in mind, in the opening years
of the twentieth century.

Now that the Mormon Church is respected
everywhere, it is hard to imagine the bitterness
with which everything Mormon was viewed in those
days. What was termed the "American Party" was
organized in Salt Lake City. This "party," composed only of those who were embittered against the
Mormons, carried on a campaign of falsehood and
defamation concerning the chief leaders of the
Church. President Smith was cartooned both in
a Utah newspaper and in periodicals published in
the East. In response to this libelous campaign,
and in contrast to it, he said this:

I feel in my heart to forgive all men in the broad sense
that God requires of me to forgive all men, and I desire
to love my neighbor as myself; and to this extent I bear no
malice toward any of the children of my Father. But there
are enemies to the work of the Lord, as there were enemies
of the Son of God. There are those who speak only evil of
the Latter-day Saints. There are those—and they abound
largely in our midst—who will shut their eyes to every virtue and to every good thing connected with this latter-day
work, and will pour out floods of falsehood and misrepre-
sentation against the people of God. I forgive them for
this. I leave them in the hands of the just Judge.

When the case came up in the Senate, in February, 1907, the motion to unseat Senator Smoot
was rejected by a vote of twenty-eight yeas and forty-
two nays; twenty senators did not vote. Thus was
justice done in the case of Reed Smoot, which was
denied in the Roberts' case.

Another reverse was experienced by members
of the Church in Mexico. It will be remembered
that, in the time of President Taylor, Mexico was
colonized by the Mormons. Since then settlements
made there increased in population, and prospered.
But in 1912 political upheavals in that country in-
terfered with the peace and safety of the Mormon
people there. They were pilfered by banditti till
it was deemed advisable for the Saints to leave
the country—at least temporarily. And they did so.
They settled on the border, in the United States,
so as to be ready, when the time came and peace
was restored, to return to their homes. Some of
them returned to Utah. In this exodus the Mormons
suffered a great loss of property.

But not all the events during this administration were of an adverse character.

In December, 1905, a monument was erected
to the Prophet Joseph Smith on the farm where he
had been born one hundred years before. This, as
the reader knows, was in Sharon, Windsor County,
Vermont. Shortly before this the farm had been

purchased by the Church, and a cottage built on the spot where the house had stood in which the Prophet was born.   The monument is a polished shaft of granite, thirty-eight and one-half feet high—one foot for each year of the Prophet's life.   Not long after this the Church also purchased the Smith farm in Manchester, New York, including the grove in which the first vision to the Prophet occurred.   And later still the Hill Cumorah was purchased by the Church, on which another monument was erected in commemoration of the coming forth of the *Book of Mormon.* These last two purchases, however, took place in the administration following that of President Smith.

A notable event was the last visit of President Smith to Europe.   With Bishop Charles W. Nibley, who was afterwards to become a member of the First Presidency, he made a tour of several countries, including England and Holland.   In Holland an eleven-year-old boy, John Roothoff, who lived in Rotterdam, was miraculously healed of blindness.

While President Smith was there, the boy said to his mother, "If you will take me with you to meeting and if President Smith will look into my eyes, I have faith that they will be made well."

The mother did so.

After the services President Smith greeted each of the members of the Church present.   When he came to the boy with a bandage over his eyes, the President raised the bandage slightly and gave the lad a blessing.

When the boy and his mother returned to their home, the lad said, "Mother, my eyes are well.   I can't feel any pain.   I can see now!"

During the seventeen years of his presidency over the Church President Smith gave wise counsel to his people, led them into some new paths of spiritual truth, and himself grew noticeably mellow and tolerant in his attitude toward friend and foe. It was a never-to-be-forgotten experience to hear him bear his testimony to the divine origin of Mormonism. Here is one of those testimonies, which he bore in 1909:

> I stand before you, my brethren and sisters and friends, on the ground that I have tried to be true to God, to the utmost of my knowledge and ability; that I have tried to be true to my people, to the utmost of my knowledge and ability; and that I have been true to the world in every pledge and promise that I have made to the world.
>
> My brethren and sisters, I know that my Redeemer lives. I know, as I know that I live, that in person he has visited man in our time and day, and that we are not dependent alone on the history of the past for the knowledge that we possess.

Chapter XXVII

THE ADMINISTRATION OF HEBER J. GRANT

Just four days after the death of President
Smith, Heber J. Grant succeeded to the presidency.
His elevation to this office took place on the twenty-
third of November, 1918. This was in accordance
with the instructions given many years before by
President Woodruff, that the re-organization of the
First Presidency should be effected as soon as pos-
sible. This advice as we have seen, was followed
in the cases of both President Snow and President
Smith. President Grant chose as his counselors Anthon
H. Lund and Charles W. Penrose, who had served in
this capacity with President Smith.

Since President Lund was the senior apostle,
after Heber J. Grant had been chosen president, he
became also president of the quorum. The vacancy created by the promotion of President Grant
was filled by the selection of Melvin J. Ballard. The
quorum then stood: Rudger Clawson, Reed Smoot,
George Albert Smith, George F. Richards, Orson F.
Whitney, David O. McKay, Anthony W. Ivins,
Joseph Fielding Smith, James E. Talmage, Stephen
L Richards, Richard R. Lyman, and Melvin J. Ballard.

Changes, however, have occurred in this quorum
during the administration of President Grant thus
far (1938.) In 1921 President Lund passed away,
and his place was taken by President Penrose,
who became first counselor; and President Penrose's place was taken by Anthony W. Ivins. The
vacancy in the quorum of Twelve thus created was
filled by the ordination of John A. Widtsoe. When
President Penrose died in 1925, President Ivins became first counselor, and Presiding Bishop Charles
W. Nibley became second counselor. Thus the First

Presidency stood till the death of President Nibley in 1931. J. Reuben Clark, Jr., was chosen second counselor in 1933. In October, 1934, President Ivins passed away, whereupon President Clark was selected first counselor, and at the same time was ordained an apostle and a member of the quorum; and

President Heber J. Grant

David O. McKay was chosen second counselor. Meantime Orson F. Whitney and James E. Talmage passed away, and the three vacancies in the quorum were filled, at different times, by the selection of Joseph F. Merrill, Charles A. Callis, and Alonzo A. Hinckley. Apostle Hinckley passed away in December, 1936, and his place was filled in April, 1937, by the ordination of Albert E. Bowen.

*   *   *   *   *

President Grant is the son of Jedediah M. Grant and Rachel Ivins. His father was counselor to President Brigham Young. President Grant was born in Salt Lake City, Utah, November 22, 1856. He is now, (1938) therefore, in his eighty-second year. But in both body and mind he is alert and active. He is the first president of the Church born in Utah. He was his mother's only child.

President Grant spent his boyhood and youth in the town of his birth—playing base ball, attending school and working for an insurance company. He also won a diploma in penmanship, and taught that subject in the University of Deseret. His early inclination being business, he became connected with a bank, where he became assistant cashier. His early reading was of the sort that proved inspirational—Smiles' *Self-help*. When sixteen years of age he read the *Book of Mormon* through. The life of Nephi, as recorded there, impressed him greatly—particularly the passage, "I know that the Lord giveth no commandments unto the children of men, save he shall prepare a way for them that they may accomplish the thing which he commandeth them." His early life was one of poverty and struggle

Religiously he has always been active. When the first Improvement Association was organized in his ward, in 1875, he was one of the assistant superintendents. Later he presided over the Tooele stake. It was from this office that he was called to the apostleship, by revelation to President John Taylor. That was in October, 1882. Until his mission to Japan, of which we have already spoken, his duties as an apostle were confined almost exclusively to the various stakes of Zion. Once, however, he and Brigham Young, Jr., went to Mexico, visiting Sonora. This was before any settlements were made there by the Mormons. Their special work was to preach the gospel to the Yaqui Indians. In 1883 and 1884 the two apostles went on a mission to the Navajo, the Moquis, the Zuni, and the Papago natives.

*   *   *   *   *

As an apostle Heber J. Grant did signal work in a financial way for the Church, the Territory of Utah, and business firms among his people.

During the financial panic of 1891 he went east and west, visiting financial interests, and obtained several hundred thousand dollars, to aid business firms that were in distress. And later, in 1893, at the request of President Woodruff, he made four trips to the East on the same errand. The President had told him he would succeed, and he did; he brought home upwards of half a million dollars for the Church and commercial institutions, and at a time when it was very difficult to induce banks to lend money.

During this same period, too, it was decided to establish the beet sugar industry in the commonwealth. Here again President Woodruff took the lead. He appointed a committee of the Twelve to study the proposed project. Heber J. Grant was a member of this committee. President Grant was also one of the organizers of the sugar company, when it was decided to effect an organization of that industry. Presently factories were built, first in Lehi and later in other parts of Utah and Idaho, to the benefit of the farmers in the commonwealth.

Moreover, President Grant has been interested in a variety of other things. He has given away one hundred thousand books to friends and acquaintances in all parts of the country. He calls this his "cigarette money." Also he is interested in art. More than one artist among his people owes his success to the encouragement of President Grant.

He has been called one of the "uncommon Americans." He is uncommon in his tall figure, in the forthrightness of his thinking and his actions, in the candor and frankness of his nature, in his generosities, in his varied interests, in the simplicity and directness of his disposition, and, above all, in his utter honesty and devotion to the work of the Lord.

*   *   *   *   *

Many interesting events have taken place in his administration, of which only the outstanding ones can be detailed in this brief history.

It was in this administration that the one hundredth anniversary of the Church's birth fell. It was a notable event, marking a century's growth. On this occasion, there was a celebration, prolonged for more than a month. The main feature was an imposing pageant, in which the various dispensations of divine providence were depicted, and in which the main events of the Last Dispensation were presented pictorially. It is estimated that more than a hundred thousand persons, Mormon and non-Mormon, witnessed this pageant.

In this administration, too, a monument was erected on the Hill Cumorah, commemorative of the coming forth of the *Book of Mormon.* It is an imposing shaft topped by a figure of the heavenly messenger, Moroni. There are also representations of some principal events connected with the appearing of the Nephite Record. The monument is placed as near as possible to the spot on which the plates of the *Book of Mormon* were buried by Moroni and obtained by the modern prophet. Near this place is a cottage where those who care to do so may obtain literature and information concerning Mormonism. Thus the story of Joseph Smith, after the lapse of a hundred years, has been fixed in enduring monuments —that on the farm where his birth took place and now on the hill where he conversed with an angel and received the plates from which came the sacred scriptures of an ancient people.

Two other significant monuments have been erected. At the old Mormon cemetery at Winter Quarters, Nebraska, the Church has raised a graphic portrayal, "The Tragedy of Winter Quarters," to the memory of the six thousand Mormon immigrants who died on the plains. On the State Capitol grounds in Salt Lake City, the Church has joined with the people of Utah in commemorating in granite and bronze the historic Mormon Battalion.

President Grant has traveled widely in preaching the restoration of the gospel. In Japan, as we have seen, in the islands of the Pacific, in Mexico, in Canada, in Europe and throughout the United States he has borne testimony of the divinity of the Latter-day work. During the summer of 1937 he revisited the European missions. The occasion was the centennial of the opening of the British mission. He called at Vauxhall in Preston, England where Heber C. Kimball and his associates first preached in 1837. Services commemorative of the first baptisms in England were held at the River Ribble. Sixteen Church-owned houses of worship were dedicated in England. The reception given the president on this occasion was in striking contrast to the unfriendly treatment accorded him as mission president some years previous.

The missions in France, Belgium, Switzerland, Germany, Czecho-Slovakia, the Netherlands, Denmark, Sweden and Norway were also visited.

Chapter XXVIII

CONCLUSION

Such, then, in brief is the history of Mormonism. We have seen how, beginning in a rural section of New York, it has gathered converts from thirty nations and set up permanent branches in widely scattered sections of the world. Organized with six members in 1830, it now counts a membership of 760,000. Once ridiculed, persecuted and driven, it has distinguished itself as a religion of unusual purpose and achievement. Many of its doctrines are singular; its history, as we have observed, is quite without parallel.

In perspective the past century presents an extraordinary picture. And now, one may ask, what of the present? In conclusion, therefore, let us examine the facts in a few phases of the varied and extensive program the Church is following today. The statistics here used are the latest available at the time of writing.

* * * * *

We have learned how on the fifteenth of May, 1829, John the Baptist conferred on Joseph Smith and Oliver Cowdery the keys of the Aaronic priesthood. Later in the same year the keys of the higher, or Melchizedek, priesthood were conferred on these two men by Peter, James and John. The Prophet and Oliver Cowdery then in turn conferred the priesthood on their immediate associates in the new ministry.

Today, through a direct line of ordination from Joseph Smith and Oliver Cowdery, more than 191,000 men and boys hold the priesthood in its various offices and officiate in its ordinances. This means that more than one-fourth of the total membership of the Church has been ordained with power to act in some official capacity. This body of men, giving voluntarily of their time, constitute the ministry of the Church. The spirit of this ministry, its manner of government, was outlined to the Prophet in a revelation received in 1839 while he was languishing in prison in Missouri.

> No power or influence can or ought to be maintained by virtue of the priesthood, only by persuasion, by long-suffering, by gentleness and meekness, and by love un-feigned . . . reproving betimes with sharpness, when moved upon by the Holy Ghost, and then showing forth afterwards an increase of love toward him whom thou hast reproved, lest he esteem thee to be his enemy.

Every man in the Church is eligible to receive the priesthood upon conditions of righteous living. It is in this vast body of authority that the strength of the organization lies.

*   *   *   *   *

Shortly after the publication of the *Book of Mormon* the Prophet's brother, Samuel, traveled about the country selling and lending copies of the book. This was perhaps the first regular missionary work done in behalf of the new cause. Since then the Church has always been a proselyting organization, and we have seen how it has grown under this stimulus.

Today there are 34 large and prosperous missions located through North and South America, Europe, South Africa, in Australia and New Zealand, and in the islands of the Pacific. Approximately 2,000 men and women, most of them young, are constantly in the field preaching the gospel by every honorable means.

They are doing this at their own expense, and at the expense of parents and friends. The monetary contribution alone of these missionaries and their families for the preaching of the gospel has

been conservatively' estimated at two million dollars
a year.

*　*　*　*　*

It will be remembered that the enlisting officer
of the Mormon Battalion was surprised to find that
every volunteer was able to sign his own name, while
only one in three of the other recruits could do so.
Latter-day Saints have always been encouraged to
take advantage of every educational opportunity.
Today illiteracy is practically nil among the Church
membership. Latter-day Saints are found on the
faculties of many American universities.

In early days schools were built and maintained
by the Church, and today a large university and
several colleges are operated. With the improvement of public school facilities in the primary and
secondary grades the Church has gradually withdrawn from secular education in those fields. However, it has always realized the desirability of religious training in connection with secular education,
and in pursuance of this ideal it has set up facilities
to fill this need. Institutes have been established in
connection with eleven universities, and seminaries
in connection with 85 high schools. In these theological training is offered along with recreational
opportunities. The manner in which such training is
received may be realized from the fact that in 1936
sixty-four per cent of the students eligible for high
school seminary work took advantage of it.

*　*　*　*　*

Without a hall in which to gather, the six original members of the Church met in Peter Whitmer's
farm house. Today, not including many halls owned
in the missions, there are more than a thousand
houses of worship wherein members of the various
ecclesiastical wards hold services. In addition there
are the temples and various other administration
buildings and auditoriums.

In connection with each ward meeting house

there is a recreation hall where facilities are provided for dramatic presentations, social dancing, and, in many cases, indoor sports. The Church has always taught the value of and sponsored wholesome recreation.

*   *   *   *   *

Provision is today made for active participation by all members from the youngest to the oldest. It has always been a principle of the Church that interest is born of individual activity. Hence a part in the ministry is available to all men. who have been ordained to office in the priesthood. Most executive positions in the Church are filled by men who pursue regular vocations, devoting their extra-vocational time to the Church. This contribution of time and talent is really tremendous. In some cases it has been estimated that there is a demand for one person in three to fill some executive or teaching position.

Opportunity for leadership and activity is afforded the women as well as the men. We have already learned that in Nauvoo the Prophet organized the Relief Society, an organization for the women of the Church, having its own officers and managing its own affairs.

Its primary purpose is to assist the needy, as one would gather from the name. However its curriculum has been broadened to include training in homemaking, the study of literature and art, and various phases of adult recreation. More than 70,000 women are enrolled in this organization.

Particularly for the youth of the Church there are the Mutual Improvement Associations, the Young Men's and the Young Women's. Boy Scout work is conducted under the direction of the Young Men's organization. The success of Scouting in the Mormon Church is attested by Dr. James E. West, Chief Scout Executive, Boy Scouts of America. He said:

Among no church which has sponsored Scouting have we met with more wholehearted and effective cooperation and generous support than in the Church of Jesus Christ of Latter-day Saints, or finer, more enthusiastic leaders of high calibre. The State of Utah has a larger percentage of Scouts in its boy population, I am told, than any other state in the Union and a larger per capita Scout membership in the Mormon faith than that of any other religious body on record.

More than 25,000 boys are today receiving Scout training under the sponsorship of the Church. In the Young Men's and Young Women's Mutual Improvemeht organizations more than 145,000 of the youth of the Church are receiving training in various fields.

For the children of the Church there exists the Primary Association to care for spiritual training and recreation. Its present membership totals nearly 100,000 boys and girls.

And then, of course, for people of all ages there is the Sunday School with a membership of more than 336,000, and a voluntary teaching corps of more than 30,000.

All of the officers and teachers in these various organizations—with the exception of a few full time directors—contribute time and effort without monetary compensation. They are drawn from the ranks of the Church. This is all part of a vast program to keep every man and woman, even every child, actively engaged in some phase of religious effort.

* * * * *

Through application of the Word of Wisdom the Church has distinguished itself as a healthy people. Temperate living and abstinence from the use of such deleterious substances as tobacco, alcohol, tea and coffee have served to build a physically sound society. Now, perhaps even to a greater extent than in early days, the leaders emphasize the value of health, and teach the Word of Wisdom as a divinely given program for healthful living.

The value of these teachings is shown in a comparison of the vital statistics of the Church with comparable statistics of the nation and the world.

At the time of writing, the birth rate of the Church was 30.6 per thousand. The death rate was only 7.2 per thousand. The net difference was 23.4 per thousand, implying unusual health and longevity. This bespeaks the effectiveness with which this teaching has been put forth by the Church.

* * * * *

We have previously discussed the manner in which in early days the Church fostered industry when it was impossible for individuals to do so. Assistance on more than one occasion was granted for projects designed for the good of the community, such as an irrigation canal or a sugar factory. In this way the people were established in industry and economic independence.

This same policy of helping people so they can better help themselves has been followed through the years. A Church Security program now provides means whereby men and women unable to find work in private industry can secure employment with which to maintain honestly themselves and their families without becoming victims of a dole.

Under this plan farms have been cultivated, mills operated, thousands of cans of foodstuffs have been preserved annually, clothing factories have been maintained, mines have been opened, and a great variety of industries promoted for the economic and moral welfare of the membership of the Church.

Thus, with leadership and cooperation the Church is today building on the foundations laid by the Prophet a program designed for the spiritual, social and economic betterment of its membership.

INDEX

●

—A—

—B—

—M—

CPSIA information can be obtained
at www.ICGtesting.com
Printed in the USA
LVHW102348210723
753016LV00003B/423